THE SUBURBAN YOU

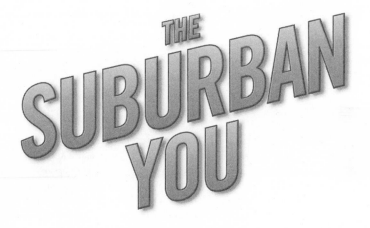

THE SUBURBAN YOU

Reports from the Home Front

MARK FALANGA

BROADWAY BOOKS • NEW YORK

PRINTED IN THE UNITED STATES OF AMERICA

BROADWAY BOOKS and its logo, a letter B bisected on the diagonal, are trademarks of Random House, Inc.

Visit our website at www.broadwaybooks.com

First edition published 2004

Book design by Chris Welch

Library of Congress Cataloging-in-Publication Data

Falanga, Mark, 1958–
The suburban you / by Mark Falanga.—1st ed.
p. cm.
ISBN 0-7679-1890-8
1. Falanga, Mark, 1958– 2. Suburbanites—United States—Biography. 3. Suburban life—Humor. I. Title.

HT352.U6F35 2004
307.74'092—dc22
2004045777

1 3 5 7 9 10 8 6 4 2

I dedicate this book to the three most important people in my life—my wife, Diane, and our kids, Blake and Bianca. After twenty years together, Diane still makes me laugh every day; she is the funniest, most honest and creative person that I know. Diane is my best friend and has a better ability to laugh at herself than anyone I have ever met in my life; without realizing it, she has supplied me with an abundance of material from which to draw upon for this book. I am so grateful for our two incredible kids, who have been so captivated with this project from the very beginning and who unknowingly prompted us to move to the suburbs and assume a lifestyle that, without them, we would have never discovered. Without the support and encouragement of Diane, Blake, and Bianca, *The Suburban You* would have never happened.

I also dedicate this book to my parents, Dolores and Sal Falanga, who taught me many things, including that if I pay attention, many funny things will reveal themselves.

ACKNOWLEDGMENTS

I would first like to acknowledge my wife, Diane. She was the first one to read this material and she laughed louder and longer than anyone. I also could not have written this book without our kids, Blake and Bianca, expressing so much interest and enthusiasm along the way and hearing them laugh at the stories I read to them. I love you all.

I thank Chris Kennedy for listening to me tell many of the stories that are in this book before it was even contemplated, over a period of several years. His laughter told me that the stories were funny. I thank Sheila Kennedy, who suggested years ago that I consider writing a book.

I thank the world's most extraordinary editor/agent/manager/mover/shaker, David Kuhn, who I believe can make anything happen. David is a guy with big ideas who delivers.

I thank Mark Bailey, who had the vision to see this material as something worthwhile and who put me in contact with David Kuhn.

I thank Jim Warren at the *Chicago Tribune,* who was the first person to publish any of my writing.

I thank the many friends and family to whom I sent the

first draft of *The Suburban You,* or who have read some of its stories and who responded with vigorous enthusiasm including: Diane, Blake, and Bianca Falanga; Dolores and Sal Falanga; Elise, Gary, Lily, and Louie Berticevich; Dolores and John Sapieta; Linda, Ed, and Julia Pucci; Pat Rehak and Jayne Tighe; Joan and Ralph Meyer; David, Terry, Jeremy, and Rachel Meyer; Linda, Elliot, Alex, Sam, and Tori Goldman; Chris and Sheila Kennedy; Max Kennedy; Mark Bailey; David Kuhn; Jim Warren; Colonel John Heller; Dick and Lorin Costolo; Ray and Marsha Pesavento; Pat and Paul Pappageorge; Art and Denise Lutschaunig; Victoria Cook; Helen Wan; Kerrie Hillman; Michael Hainey; Chris Knutsen; Nina Willdorf; Walter Bode; Doug Seibold; Robbie Deveney; Richard Rubin; Jennifer and Scott Woolford; Michael and Pat Welborn; Greg and Lianne Mech; Karen DeMar; Frank Zinn and Lauren Isenberg-Zinn; Jodi Coe; Joan and Steve Ulrich; Jim and Lisa Carlton; Woo Holmberg; John Kupper and Janet Koestring; Mark and Wendy Irwin; JJ Hanley; Jim Kokoris; Dana and Janet Olsen; Debbie Regina; Steven Levy; Linda Stremmel; Sky Geyer; Ann-Marie Farley; Sean Bisceglia; Julie Stahl; Barb Dunlap; Matt Walker; and Tina James.

I thank Deb Futter, Bill Thomas, David Drake, John Fontana, Michael Windsor, and Anne Merrow at Doubleday Broadway, who are the most creative and fun group of book publishers to work with anywhere.

CONTENTS

PROLOGUE

Living in the coolest part of the city, you never imagined yourself ever living in the suburbs. Then you have a kid. He starts to get bigger and older. Soon you recognize fewer and fewer familiar faces at the parks that you frequent with your kid, the same parks where, only a year or two earlier, you knew everyone. You recognize fewer people because those familiar faces have moved to the suburbs. They sold out.

You start looking at houses in the suburbs and are horrified at the thought of living there. Then you meet some people who live there and they like it. They show you some of the fun suburban stuff to do. It takes you awhile, but you acquire a taste for vintage homes and brick streets, which at first looked old and run-down but now look charming to you.

Your kid will be ready for kindergarten next year and your options are some low-rung city public school or one of two $15,000+++ private schools where kids do not know how to catch a football or ride a two-wheeled bike.

You find a house in the suburbs and you move there. You, my man, are living in the suburbs with your family. Over time, you come to realize that you did the best thing for your family and can admit that you have entered a new phase of your life, the suburban you.

YOUR SUBURBAN TRANSITION

Help Your Wife Decide If She Should Work or Not

You live in the city and your wife has a nice career going, as a corporate executive with a shampoo company. She likes her job and is engaged in her work. As a side benefit, she has a great excuse for talking about hair, one of her favorite topics. Then one day, after you have sex, she is pregnant. Her belly gets big and she delivers a baby in a hospital where they tell you to put on hospital scrubs over underwear you are not wearing.

In three months, your wife resumes her career. You hire the nanny that she selects and you think that everything is going the way that makes your wife happiest. Except for one problem: every single day, your wife comes home from work crying. Not a little sniffle but a full-fledged, all-out fifteen-minute sob.

Each and every day, you ask her what is wrong. "Why are you crying?" you ask, and she tells you the same thing. She says, "I like working, but I want to stay home with Blake." You are fortunate that either scenario is an option. So every single day for two years you say, "Honey, you do what will make you happy."

The next day, and every Monday through Friday thereafter,

you will relive this same scenario. It lasts about fifteen to twenty minutes each evening. Your feeling on this matter is crystal clear. You believe that there is nothing more important than your kid, and that the right thing is for your wife to stay home with him. You, however, do not want to reveal this opinion to her, because you feel even more strongly that this difficult decision is hers to make. The best answer, you believe, is the one that will make her happiest.

One day, your wife comes home and announces that she has made a decision. She is clear, she says, and she has inner peace. She wants to stay home. You say, "Whatever will make you happy, honey."

Except that the next day, when she comes home, she tells you that she will continue working. You reply, "Whatever will make you happy, honey."

Then one day for real she makes her decision and the next day announces it to her colleagues. That, you and your son believe, is the best decision that she has ever made, and, by the way, she has never cried again—about that.

Next stop, the suburbs.

Move to the Suburbs

You have spent three or four nights a week, or so it seems, over the past year and a half looking for a house in the suburbs. In the last month or so you have really ramped up your search for a suburban home because you had sex again and you just found out that your wife is pregnant with your second child. Alone, you leave your city house, while your wife stays at home with your child. You leave when your son goes to bed, usually between 8 and 10:30 P.M., a time that you are never able to predict, because with your first child you did not want to interfere with his natural sleep patterns (a philosophy that, by the way, your wife turned 180 degrees on with your daughter, your second child). From where you live in the city, you drive the half hour up to the North Shore suburbs, where you think you will live, because there you are close to the lake and your kids can go to the best schools around. They are public schools, and kids there know what a football is and can ride two-wheeled bikes.

You make this trek many evenings, armed with listings of properties that are for sale and a suburban map, which you have marked in advance, noting the exact location of each property. You arrange the listing sheets in the order in which you will drive by the homes that are for sale, so that you can perform this thankless task in as short a time frame as possible, so that you can get home and go to sleep, so that you can wake up refreshed and ready to be a corporate executive tomorrow.

Your task is to drive by each house and see if you can find one that you can imagine you and your family living in. You think that this task should not take that long, given the amount of money you are willing to pay for a house, but you are wrong. You are wrong because everything you look at looks so old and run-down. At the time, you are living in a four-story, contemporary city house. It is large and clean, and was new when you moved in. While you are stepping up in your purchase price-wise, it doesn't seem that way house-wise. You think that in the price range you are looking at you should be able to find a house on a hill, overlooking the lake, with a nice spread of land. And the house should ramble. You think that such a house should exist, but you are dead wrong. Rather, the houses are old-looking, they are on small lots, and they all need hundreds of thousands of dollars of work. This, you come to accept, is the price you pay for brick streets, big trees, living close to the lake, having smart neighbors who are interesting, and access to really good schools.

The brokers who assist you in this process are generally really old ladies. They are not like you and your wife at all; in fact, being old and being out of touch seem to be the two main characteristics of the brokers with whom you align yourself. These are brokers who were last in the city you are moving from twenty-five years ago, and whose main qualification is their tenure in living in the suburbs where you are looking.

You tell them, in great detail, the characteristics of a house and street that will appeal to you, but they keep on sending you listing sheet after listing sheet of properties that don't even come close. You invite them to your city house and try your best to articulate what you want, but they send you to see the opposite. You up your upper limit by a few hundred thousand dollars, but it makes no difference in what you see. The houses all need so much work and they were all designed for the way families lived eighty years ago, however that was.

This routine becomes redundant, until one day your friend-boss says to you, "Why don't you give Megan O'Connor a call?" You do and you find out that she lived where you live in the city and she knows your scene. She is young, like you, and she gets it. You ask Megan to please call your wife so that your wife can articulate to her what you want in a house and a neighborhood. They talk and Megan says, "There is a house that just came on the market that I think you will like." Your wife says OK and you meet Megan at the house that evening after work.

You drive up to the house and you and your wife look at each other and know that this is the one that you will buy. You walk through it and it is funky; it has personality and character, and a large yard with big trees. It is close to the lake and the schools and is on a brick street that many call gracious, because the houses are set so far back from the road.

You tour the house, you accept that you will want to do extensive work on it, and you walk out. You and your pregnant wife talk on the lawn and you tell Megan that you will buy that house. Your wife says that there is no better house for your family and that she would like this house. "This is the one," she says. Later that evening, after your broker's office has closed, you submit a signed contract and drop it in the mail slot on the front door of your broker's office. It falls to the floor. You and your wife are happy. This issue is behind you.

Until that night, that is. Your wife, at two o'clock in the morning, wakes up crying. "I don't want to move!" she cries. "I don't like that old house." You know that your wife does not like change, even in small doses. For God's sake, she is still using a 1984 Macintosh SE. She is so upset that you say, "The only thing that we can do is retrieve the contract that I dropped off at Megan's office earlier this evening. Because nobody was there, I slipped it in the mail slot, and we can fish it out," you say, trying to comfort her.

You go to the basement of your home and craft a stick with a nail on the end of it to poke your contract and direct it out of the mail slot. You and your new tool will go to the real-estate office at 5 A.M., before any of the brokers get in on Saturday morning. Your plan is to retrieve the contract, which nobody will even know you have submitted. You take a drive up to the office and your contract is not on the floor, under the mail slot, where you last saw it. You see it on the receptionist's desk and it is clearly out of reach of you and your new tool. You return to your car and like an FBI surveillance agent you stake out this office until someone arrives. You prepare yourself for what may be a four-hour surveillance but hope that it is less. You cannot believe that this is happening.

At 7:10 on that Saturday morning, someone enters the office and you step out of your car and follow him in. You reach for the envelope with your contract in it and slip it into your pocket. You then pretend that you want some information on a particular listing, so you ask the person whom you followed into the office if he has any information on 1103 Sycamore Street. You take a listing sheet that you have no interest in and leave without engaging in any further conversation. The contract that you came to intercept is now safely concealed in the inner breast pocket of your jean jacket.

Over the weekend, you have several discussions with your wife. The first one centers on the fact that you and she have been looking at houses for a year and a half. "Why," you ask, "did you think that we were going through with this exercise? Did it ever occur to you that all this would conclude one day with us actually finding a house that we wanted to live in?" Surprisingly, your wife admits to you that she was not prepared for actually *finding* a house that she would like. You agree that the neighborhood is everything you want. It is quaint, peaceful, and quiet, and has character. The house is the most suitable that you have seen. She is ready to go through with it. You tell her that you are submitting the contract and that you will not retrieve it. Two months later, you close on the purchase of your new house.

Five months after buying the house, you are well under way with the renovation and you are ready to put your city house on the market. You engage another broker, who one day puts a For Sale sign outside of your city house. For the past five months your wife has understood that you were committed to the new house; you bought it, and are doing work on it, and you assumed as part of that process she understood that you would eventually sell your city house. However, understanding all of that does not prevent your wife from crying hysterically the day that she comes home to a For Sale sign posted in front of your city house. "What were you thinking?" you ask, as gently as you can. You let this one slide.

You are eager to get the work done in your new home, because there are things that are more fun in life than paying for two homes when the second one is not in Telluride, Jackson Hole, or Crested Butte. The work is completed just two months late, and you move in January, two and a half months after your daughter is born and after selling your city home.

That first weekend in your new home, before you are even unpacked, you invite friends from the city over one evening. You tell them about the brick streets, the big trees, and the proximity to the beach. You tell them how quiet and how peaceful it is in your new neighborhood. "It is so quaint," you say. "A real safe neighborhood." "Everyone here is so nice," you say. "We have brick streets." They have no interest in any of this. They are thinking that you sold out. You have abandoned them and there is nothing that you can say about it that will change their already made-up minds.

Then John asks, "Hey, what is that orange glow outside? Is someone barbecuing or something?" It is a cold, snowy January night, and it would surprise you if someone were barbecuing, but maybe this is what they do in the suburbs, you think, to justify the expense of those built-in barbecue grills. You walk over to the dining-room window, and standing outside your next-door neighbor's side door is a kid who looks like he is twelve years old. He is holding a homemade contraption that consists of an in-line bicycle pump and a reservoir of some sort. He is furiously pumping this in-line bike pump and napalm is shooting out of it. You look in disbelief as you realize that your next-door neighbor's twelve-year-old kid has built a flamethrower, which works spectacularly well. The kid is shooting fifteen-foot flames from this sophisticated homemade device, and he is enjoying it more than he should be. He is mesmerized, and so are you and your jaded city friends, who thought until tonight that they had seen everything.

You, your wife, your friend, and his wife are all looking out the window, not knowing what to say. You imagine the value of your house has dropped by 40 percent tonight and that you selected the one house in the entire suburb that is next door to a twelve-year-old pyromaniac. On top of that, you have lost all credibility with your city friends, who will no longer believe you when you tell them how idyllic your suburban life is. You know they can't wait to pass this story on to all of your other city friends who also think that you sold out.

After you witness this, you tell them that despite the fact that you live next to a twelve-year-old pyromaniac you still live on a brick street. After five minutes or so of vigorous flamethrowing, your new twelve-year-old neighbor makes eye contact with the four of you staring at him and runs inside. Now you are concerned that he will get the big-momma flamethrower and that he will start testing it out on your recently acquired shingle-style house. "Welcome to the suburbs," your friends say. "We love the brick streets, they are so quaint. You made a great choice. It will be so much safer here than in the city for the kids."

Say Goodbye to Your City Accountant

When you lived in the city, you became a client of an accountant to whom your friend Bill Smith referred you. Your accountant's name is Brian, and he lives with his wife. You think that he told you that he was forty years old or so. Brian and his wife do not have children, but they have a big dog that intimidates you every time you visit Brian at tax time. You deal with it because Brian is a good accountant and you like the fact that he works out of his home and is not part of some Big 10, Big 8, Big 6, or whatever type of accounting firm it is that charges you hundreds of dollars an hour to support their big whatever overhead.

You have worked with Brian for several years, and you like that. It is a theme that runs through your life. You like stable relationships. You like that he knows you and your record-keeping well enough that you no longer have to explain every little line item to him. He owns a few buildings and you like that, because you do, too, and you think that he knows how to position you in the most tax-advantaged way to the IRS.

Brian looks like an accountant. If you ran into Brian somewhere and you did not know him and someone asked you,

"What do you think that guy does?" you would respond that you think that he is an accountant. Why? Well, Brian is pasty-looking, summer and winter. You are not sure if he goes outside at all. You have seen him in T-shirts and you would say that he lacks muscle definition. You would also say that he has a paunch. It is not a beer belly, because you are not sure if Brian drinks beer. If he does, you think it would be out of a glass, not a bottle.

Brian waddles when he walks and his voice is a little nasal, like a good accountant's voice should be. His fingernails need trimming and they are dirty. He is methodical in his approach to everything.

You see him as rather asexual. He talks about his wife, but you have never ever seen her. She works at Kraft, you are told, and is a corporate executive. It all fits, but sometimes you wonder if he really does have a wife or if this is just a fabrication for the benefit of his tax clients. On this topic, you have even gone so far as to think that perhaps all of Brian's talk about his "wife" is a way for him to justify, in case he has to someday, taking a larger tax deduction by filing a joint return. This point about Brian's wife is one that you will never bring clarity to.

The other interesting thing about Brian is that you have never seen him wear shorts, not even on the hottest summer days. You usually see him in the winter, and his house is as hot as your nana's New York City apartment used to be. You keep your billable discussions with Brian brief, not because you are concerned with getting overbilled but because you are so frigging hot that you can't stand it. Once you asked Brian if he would mind opening a window and you knew by his facial expression that he did not think it was a good idea. You never asked again.

This year, you pick up your completed tax forms, with all the envelopes addressed and affixed with the proper postage (you love those envelopes and the postage, and that, alone, was enough to keep you coming back to Brian). Your tax forms are thicker than usual, because they include additional schedules for selling your city house and buying your suburban home.

When you pick up your forms Brian announces that this will be his last year doing your taxes. You wonder if you offended him that time when you asked him to open a window, or maybe he just doesn't like suburban clients, now that you are one. You hesitantly ask why. Brian tells you that he and his "wife" are moving. It is 8 P.M. and his wife is not there.

"Where are you moving to?" you ask Brian. He tells you he is moving to Southern California. "Southern California, that sounds nice," you say, as you imagine Brian as the whitest, pastiest, least muscle-defined male in all of Southern California. You have a hard time seeing the connection. You were expecting his response to be something more like "Cleveland."

"Where in Southern California?" you ask, to which he responds, "Palm Springs." You do not know much about Palm Springs, except that every winter your father-in-law and his new wife go to a place called Rancho Mirage, where he plays golf all day, every day. You think of Rancho Mirage in Palm Springs and you imagine a bunch of old people playing golf all the time. You recall your father-in-law telling you that there are more golf courses per capita or per acre or per something in Palm Springs than anywhere else. But you are not so sure that you are really referencing the right place, because you get Palm Springs confused with Palm Something-or-Other in Florida, or maybe it's The Palms in Nevada. Who knows?

"Why are you moving out there?" you ask, a bit surprised, because it seems to you that Brian has built up a healthy pool of clients over the several years that you have worked with him. You know that you have personally referred several people to him. And you assume that his "wife" has a good thing going at

Kraft or Nabisco, wherever it is that she does her corporate-executive thing. He responds, "We bought a hotel." "No shit," you say. A hotel, this is serious, you think. He replies, "Well, it is a small boutique hotel; it's not such a big deal." People always say that when they sense that you sense that they are doing something cooler than you are.

For the first time, you get interested in this conversation and make the transition from being conversationally polite to really being interested in what your pasty-white, no-muscle-definition accountant is telling you.

You also note that Brian is loath to offer up any information on his own. He is polite and will answer any question that you pose to him, but he will not be forthcoming on his own. You keep on priming the pump. "So who stays at the hotel? Will it be people vacationing and playing golf?" On this he elaborates in more detail. He tells you that Palm Springs has an older golf culture, which is very strong. But you also have heard that there is a substantial gay community there as well. "And who is your target market?" you ask, as a polite way of ascertaining which choir Brian really sings in. He responds, "Well, this is a niche hotel. It is unique. The name of it is the Clayton Inn. It is an historic hotel that has a colorful past and has been around for a while." For the first time, he offers an unsolicited response: "Marilyn Monroe used to stay there." "No kidding," you say.

"What niche is it that you are pursuing with this hotel?" you ask. "Well, the hotel has an interesting history. It is a nudist hotel." To this, your jaw drops and your eyes pop out of your head. This is news that you cannot wait to get home and tell your wife. Your pasty-white, overweight, no-muscle-definition, nerdy, dirty and long fingernailed, hot-temperature-loving, long-pants-wearing accountant is buying a nudist hotel with his invisible, corporate-executive wife. Brian, you come to realize, is a self-actualized guy operating at the pinnacle of Maslow's hierarchy pyramid.

You digest that last piece of information that Brian has offered. Brian looks at your surprised expression and then corrects himself, not wanting to leave you with a misimpression. "Well," he says, "it is clothing-optional."

"Are the guests young? Old? Do they play golf?" you ask. The answer is yes to all of this. "The guests include anyone who wants to go to a nude hotel," Brian tells you. You guess that no one from your suburb is familiar with this hotel.

Too anxious to get home to tell your wife, you get up and wish Brian the absolute best with his new endeavor. Then you race home to tell the story to your wife, who you know will be able to tell it better than you to all of your friends who know or know of Brian.

Meet Your Across-the-Street Neighbor

Your suburb, like most, is a suburb of families. In each and every house there resides a family. When couples become empty-nesters, they move out of your suburb to a luxurious condo somewhere and a family with young kids buys their house for more money than you can possibly imagine. Everyone you see is a mom, a dad, or a kid. Well, almost everyone.

There is a house across the street from you that you have heard is occupied by an older woman. She spends half the year in England, so you have heard, and while she is out of the country she likes someone in her house, so she brings in a house-sitter.

One day, you are out on the front lawn playing baseball with your kid and from the house across the street emerges a tall, beautiful, young, blond-haired European-looking woman wearing short tight shorts and a tank top. Her flat stomach is exposed and it looks good. She does not look like a mom, but the funny thing is she does not look like a kid, either. She looks like she would be in between the two.

You are puzzled. You are also a friendly neighbor, and on this day you pull out all the stops to be the absolute friendliest neighbor you know how to be. You are mostly thinking of teaching your son how a good neighbor should act and behave when meeting a new neighbor. This is the perfect opportunity to teach your son the finer points of suburban neighborly etiquette. You really want to make your new neighbor feel comfortable and welcome, especially because she is young, tall, blond, and thin, has an angular face, wears tummy-exposing tank tops, and looks like she will speak with an accent like one of your best friends, who is Swedish.

"Hello," you say, loud enough to carry across the street and to penetrate any possible language barrier. "My name is Mark, and this is my son, Blake. We live here." You point to the house whose front lawn you are standing on. "We are your neighbors," you declare proudly, thinking that the benefits of living across the street from this neighbor are enough to offset the 40 percent reduction in your home's value as a result of living next door to a twelve-year-old pyrotechnician. Soon your hypothesis about your new neighbor is confirmed. She is, in fact, neither a mom nor a kid: she is Annika and she is from Sweden. In your introductory meeting, you learn that Annika is a swim teacher at your gym. Your son likes to swim, and in fact Annika looks like she would be a wonderful swim teacher for him, especially when you imagine her immersed in water wearing a Swedish bathing suit. To you, she looks like such a great teacher that you set up lessons for your son right there on the spot. Not weekday lessons either, no way. Bringing your son to swim lessons is a dad's job, you convince yourself. Besides, you do not want to burden your wife with this job, since she is already so, so busy. She will appreciate that you are trying to ease her burden and she may even reward you for it. Your son will have Saturday swim lessons just so that you can watch his progress.

Each Saturday, you faithfully bring your son to his swim

lesson with Annika. You show up early on most Saturdays to make sure that your son is not late, and oh, by the way, you go down to the pool while Annika is wrapping up her prior lesson. You insist that your son take his swim lessons in the coldest of the three pools to toughen him up a bit.

At the next block party, you ask your neighbor Bill if he has yet met Annika, his new next-door neighbor. He asks if you are talking about the tall, good-looking, angular-faced blond Swede who sunbathes nude in her backyard. He then responds, "No, we have not officially 'met,' but I have *seen* her." At that moment, you realize that you and your ex-accountant Brian now have more in common than you ever thought.

Being the good neighbor that you are, you ask Bill if you can check up on his house while he is on summer vacation in August. You are concerned that if one of his water pipes bursts his house will flood. You are concerned that his house look lived-in to deter the criminals that are so prevalent in your high-end suburb.

Do Some Shopping for Your Wife

It has been a tough week, because both your wife and your daughter have been sick for most of it. It is the weekend, and because of this sickness you know that you will not get the things done that you would like to get done. On Sunday, your wife gives you a list. Even when she is sick with pneumonia, your wife has the wherewithal to be extremely detailed in making her list. In working off of your wife's list, there is no margin for you to make any creative selections, or equal or better substitutions. Not that you do these shopping trips with any frequency, but you accept the fact that, when you do, you will bring home something that is entirely a mistake, in your wife's mind, even though, in your mind, it is on the list and is exactly what your wife wanted.

You finish up at the grocery store and head over to the Eton Paint store. Two weeks ago, your wife commenced the project of changing the color of the seventy-square-foot ceiling in your kids' bathroom, a project that you thought would take an hour and cost $75. You already did a major renovation of your suburban home before you moved in, and now the white bathroom ceiling, which was fine before, is just not the right color.

You came home on the evening when the project should have been completed to take a look at the new ceiling color and what you saw was that half of your kids' bathroom ceiling had been torn out. Apparently, when the painter came he found that there was a leak in the bathroom above the kids' bathroom, causing the ceiling to get damp. There were two possible causes for the ceiling dampness, the painter told your wife: a leaking pipe and/or the shower surround, which might need to be regrouted.

Your wife had the grouter come in first, and that job, with the upgrade to epoxy grout—not the grout that everyone else uses—cost $705. You are sure that if you lived in another suburb the cost would have been $205. After the grout job, your wife brought in the local suburban plumber. He inspected the bathroom and told your wife that there was a leak. Your wife told you that the plumber told her that they would charge $90 per hour to fix it and that they thought they could do it in a day. You do the math and realize that the plumber your wife brought in is making $180,000 per year, assuming no overtime. You insist on another plumber. The next plumber comes in, the one who did the plumbing on your house renovation in the first place, and he completes the job for $400. "It's a great deal," your wife tells you. "We saved $320." You are already $1,105 into this project and you still have half of your bathroom ceiling torn out. Another $500 to go, you estimate.

At Eton Paint, your task is to pick up the paint that your wife has selected for the ceiling. She gives you a Post-it note with the following information:

Eton Paint
HC 79
Greenbrier Beige
Kitchen & Bath
Satin

Across the note your wife has written "33.94," which you assume is the price that Eton Paint has told her they will charge. You go to the Eton Paint store where you have purchased all of the paint that you buy for your home and all of the buildings that you own. The Eton Paint store that you go to is in Southington, the suburb to your immediate south; you must have purchased more than fifty gallons of paint there over the past year.

You show the note that your wife has written for you to the Eton paint expert behind the counter and he looks it over. He is OK until he gets to the word "satin." He tells you that HC 79 is a Benjamin Moore paint and that Benjamin Moore satin is an oil-based paint, and unless you are painting an existing coat of oil paint it is the wrong paint. You need a pearl finish, he says, if you want latex paint. "Do you know if you need oil or latex?" he asks.

Because you painted the bathroom yourself the last time it was painted you know for a fact that it is latex. That time, the job took you forty-five minutes to complete, including the ten minutes it took you to find the paint roller, and cost you a total of $43.27. In your life, you have never painted or specified that anything requiring painting be painted in anything other than latex. You and he are puzzled, trying to figure out why your wife has written "satin" on the Post-it note. The other thing that puzzles you and him is the number 33.94. It does not have a dollar sign in front of it, but you and he assume it to be the price of a gallon of paint. However, he does not have any paint in his entire inventory that matches that price. He tells you that your wife must have made a mistake when she wrote that down. You doubt that—not your wife, the list-maker.

At that point, you ask him if you can use the store's phone, because you left your cell phone in the car. You call your wife to try to bring clarity to this issue and you let the phone ring at least twenty times. You have call-waiting and caller ID on your home phone and an answering machine that kicks in after four rings. What is going on, you conclude, is that your wife has prioritized whomever she is talking with over you. She knows that you are at Eton Paint picking up the paint, but she will not answer your call. You know that the caller ID says "Eton Paint" when you call, and you know that she has looked at the caller ID while on the phone, like she does each and every time you see her talking on the phone with someone when another call comes in. You also know that each of the twenty times or so that you let the phone ring the phone on her end makes an annoying clicking sound, designed to remind her that someone, in this case her husband, is trying to reach her from Eton Paint.

You expect a call back to the store, so you tell the paint expert, with confidence, that you are sure your wife will call back. You wait, but she does not. You call again five minutes later and the same thing happens: again, you let the phone ring at least twenty times, but the call that your wife is on, you guess, is too important to interrupt for you.

The paint expert looks at you for direction as to what to do. You make the decision to move ahead. The paint that you are purchasing is $36.95, yet your wife has "33.94" written on the paper. You convince the paint expert to sell the paint to you for the price that your wife wrote down.

You arrive home with the bags of groceries and you put everything away, trying to pitch in and help as much as possible while your wife is ill. You put the can of paint on the kitchen counter and twenty minutes later Eton Paint calls, a call that your wife answers immediately after looking at the caller ID, which reads "Eton Paint." While asking you why Eton Paint is calling, but before you respond, she answers the phone after two rings and says, "My husband was just there. He has the paint and it is here." She hangs up and she is upset. She cannot believe how badly you screwed up. "Where did you go to pick up the paint?" she asks. You tell her that you went to Eton Paint, the one that you always go to, in Southington. "I ordered the paint at the Eton Paint in *Northington*, not Southington," she tells you, a store that you did not know even exists.

"The Northington store custom-mixed the paint that you were supposed to pick up," she tells you. "Now we will have to pay $34 for paint that we don't need." She cannot fathom having to pay $34 for an extra gallon of paint on this ceiling paint job, which has already cost $1,105 and will likely cost more than $1,600 when it is done.

You think that you could probably talk the Northington Eton Paint store out of having to pay the $34, and if you can't you understand that that $34 represents about 2 percent of the money that you have so far invested in this project and, by the time the project is done, will represent little more than 1 percent. The worst-case scenario is that you have an extra $34 gallon of paint in the house, even if it is a custom color. You have absorbed larger-scale losses than this, that you know for a fact.

You call the Northington Eton Paint guy back and tell him that you went to the Southington store by mistake because you did not know there was a store in Northington. He tells you that there is no problem. "Don't worry about it," he says. "Happens all the time."

For some reason that you do not wish to explore, your wife is still upset with you, like you went out and intentionally bought her the incorrect paint at the wrong store and inconsiderately ignored her wishes, just to mess with her. Your wife then looks at the paint that you brought home and it says "Pearl Finish." You explain to her what the Eton Paint expert told you, that satin is oil-based and that it is incompatible with the preexisting latex that is on the ceiling now. You sound authoritative. She is not convinced by your explanation, and now she is upset that you have the right color but a finish that is pearl instead of satin.

She is mad at you again, and this time she is really mad. She is upset because the painter is coming in just seventeen hours, and that she will not have the correct materials for him to work with. Horror stories of buying an extra gallon of paint resurface in your wife's mind.

You call over to the Eton Paint Northington store to tell him about the paint that you were given by the expert in the Southington store. He describes to you that there is an anti-mold formula in the paint that you should have, but it is not in the pearl-finish paint that you have in your possession. You ask if you can switch out the pearl paint you have for the satin gallon that he mixed. He says, "Yes, no problem." You drive over to the store and get the perfect paint, the paint that should restore your wife's happiness.

With the paint issue resolved, your wife is now ready to move on to the next thing that is upsetting her, the Post Grape-Nuts that you brought home, which are not the Kellogg's Crunchy Nuggets that she specified. You hope that your wife feels better really soon.

Pay Your Bills

Now you decide to paint the exterior of your house and you go out and get a few quotes to make sure you are getting the best possible price available. You find two painters through a free weekly city newspaper in which you believe you will find the names of painters who have not done much work in the suburbs and who have not yet figured out what most of the painters who paint houses in your suburbs have figured out: that they can add a massive upcharge for doing work for people who have the capacity to pay for it.

To confirm your theory about this, you get quotes from two suburban painters whom you find in the phone book. Their quotes are three and five times the quotes of the highest city painter, and five and seven times the lowest city painter.

You hire the city guy with the lowest quote, because you think that painting is painting and that you can get your house painted seven times over for the amount of money that the most expensive suburban painter wants to paint it once.

The painter shows up Monday with his crew and he begins to paint your house.

On Saturday, as he is finishing his work, you are talking with him about the job he has done. You compliment him. He has done a fine job and you are feeling smart for hiring him. As you are talking with him, he slips in a story that is unrelated to anything that you have ever talked about with him. He tells you that he was painting a house, located at 6830 West Center Street, in the city, and that he did not get paid for the job. After the job was completed, he called, stopped by a few times, and even wrote a letter to the homeowner to get his final payment. It never came.

One Tuesday, after a month of this, the painter goes to a place called "the Pool," in the city, where temporary laborers stand early in the morning to be hired by the day by contractors and others looking for temporary help. It is an informal labor pool and it works for everyone.

Your painter rounds up three of the strongest-looking guys standing there and gives them each a crisp $100 bill. He tells them that he has a rush garage-demolition project and that by 4 P.M. the freshly painted two-car frame garage located behind 6830 West Center Street must be leveled to the ground. "Just throw all the debris in the backyard," the painter directs, "and you can have anything that was left inside." These are his parting comments to the three strong men that he hired.

That Saturday, before your painter has completed the paint job on your house, you cut him his final payment and then some.

Get New Towels for Your House

You are a guy who likes a quick shower. Like eating, showering is something that, for you, is a task to be completed as quickly as possible. It is not a recreational activity to be enjoyed. To you, the process of showering takes time away from doing the things that you enjoy doing, like hanging out with your family and looking at buildings to buy.

You want to take your shower, get out of the shower, dry off, shave, put on some deodorant, get dressed, and go. You are in control of this process and you have it down to five minutes—that is, until your wife buys new towels for the master bathroom.

Your favorite towels are the ones that you "inadvertently" brought home from the gym on a few occasions. They are small, they are plain white, and they dry you faster and better than anything else that you would call a towel in your home.

Finding these small, plain white towels that you like so much is oftentimes a struggle, as your wife does not like the way they look. To her, they look like what they are—gym towels. They do not fit in with your master-bath décor, she would say. "Out of sight, out of mind" is her philosophy when it comes to the towels that you like because they dry you so well. Her solution to what she perceives as your towel problem is to go out and buy new towels, ones that will, as she sees it, be visually compatible with the aesthetic theme of the master bathroom, whatever that is.

In the nineteen years that you have known your wife, she has had this knack for buying new towels that do not dry you. It is not as though she buys new towels frequently, but every time she does she buys ones that fail to dry. When she buys the towels, she does not think to inquire as to how the towels will dry you, nor does she look to see what material the towels are made of. Rather, her focus is purely on the visual attributes of the towels. "Will the herringbone pattern of the towel complement the texture and color of the new epoxy tile grout?" you imagine her to be asking herself as she is deciding between one nondrying towel pattern and another. You hope these new towels are not the spark of inspiration that will lead her to make a $1,600-plus bathroom-ceiling color change in *your* bathroom.

One morning after your shower, you notice the new towels, the ones with the herringbone pattern. You reach for one unexcitedly, because you have been the victim of your wife's new towels before. You slide the towel over your body and you are still damp, no matter how much you rub either side of the towel over yourself.

You open up the sink-base cabinet to find your gym towels, the ones that you know will dry you, but they have been moved to a location that you know you will never guess. You have no option other than to do your best with the new towel.

After spending twice as long to dry off as you usually do, you complete your shave and rely on your suit pants and starched white shirt to complete the drying process. You try to brush off the new towel fuzz that has affixed itself to your face, but it does not want to let go. You will work on that on the train ride in.

The next morning, you take your shower downstairs because your shower has just been regrouted and is drying. You know that the basement bathroom towels dry you reliably, and for this the hassle of walking downstairs to take a shower is worthwhile. You take your shower and reach for a towel, only to realize it is a towel that you have never seen before. Your wife, in addition to upgrading the upstairs towels, has changed the basement towels as well.

Tomorrow you look forward to taking your shower at the gym.

Have Your Relatives Visit

Your parents are in their mid-seventies and they live in a suburb of San Francisco. They moved there from a suburb of New York. They are retired and have a pretty good life. Your father, a retired Wall Street banker, has had some minor complications with his health, like a stroke, five-way bypass surgery, getting hit by a car and breaking his leg, and a few other things that you are unable to remember. He has pulled through all of this miraculously well and, besides getting a little confused every once in a while, he is pretty much like he was. Your mother is a saint in dealing with your father's ailments. She has flow, and you believe that it is from her that you have acquired your flow and your ability to laugh at everyday things.

Your parents enjoy visiting you and your family, and are excited to see your new eighty-three-year-old suburban home for the first time, now that the kids' bathroom ceiling is the right color and the herringbone-patterned master-bath towels match the $705 epoxy grout. They even come in the winter, which surprises you because they have quickly gotten acclimated to that California weather, where they define anything below fifty degrees as cold. Like many Californians, they enjoy talking about the weather to you in the winter, when they know that it is five degrees below zero where you live and seventy degrees where they live. They are in a competition that you will lose every time.

The way that you can tell that your father has had a massive stroke, a five-way bypass, a broken leg, and some other stuff that you can't quite remember is that when he comes to your house to visit, things happen to him that never happened to him before all that. During their visit, your father is sporting hearing aids, which he has never worn before. Growing up, your father frequently responded with "What?" to many things that were said, and when he watched TV it was always too loud for you and the rest of your family, so you all left the room. You, your sister, and your mother would tell your father that he should have his hearing checked and get a hearing aid. To which he would respond, "What?" When he finally understood what you were talking about, he would shake his head no, indicating that there were no deficiencies with his hearing. Finally, at seventy-five, he has heeded this advice, mostly coming from your mother, who at this point, day in and day out, was having to yell everything to him just so he could hear her.

The hearing aids that your father purchased are the high-tech ones, the ones with $100 batteries that need to be changed every two months. Your frugal father keeps his hearing aids turned down low in order to preserve the life of his batteries and thereby save energy and money. The downside is that when they are turned down so low he cannot hear, but the upside is that by doing this he extends the life of his batteries for another half a month. So, rather than hearing things clearly for two months before the batteries need to be changed, he chooses *not* to hear things for two and a half months, and he saves $120 a year on batteries.

These hearing aids make a high-pitched sound when they

are not adjusted correctly, which is most of the time. The sound is annoying and can be heard by everyone except your father, because he has his hearing aids turned down so low. It is the sound that you imagine a dog whistle would make, if you could hear such a thing. When this happens, you and everyone else calls your father's attention to it, but he fails to be convinced that there is anything wrong. He will not even acknowledge that this annoying sound is originating from him; he is convinced that it is coming from your suburban home.

Your father has a bit of a hard time with technology. He grew up in a world where most things that required controlling were controlled manually, not electronically. Video players and computers are confusing to him. So are house alarms. When you bought your house, you inherited a house alarm, and you try *not* to activate it when your parents visit. And, just in case you do, you change the access code to 1111 while they are in town so that everyone can remember and use it, if necessary. You give everyone instructions about how to open the door and then walk to the keypad and enter 1111 to deactivate the alarm. You demonstrate this to everyone, even though you know there will be no circumstance when the alarm is set and no occasion when either of your parents will be entering the house alone.

Your alarm system is tied in to the police department, and, while it has never been tested, you assume that when the alarm goes off the police will show up. You are not quite sure how this connection works, but you do understand that you pay $48.32 per month for it. One Saturday, your father decides to go for a walk. He wants to go alone, to challenge himself to see if he can find his way back home easily, like he would be able to before having a stroke, a heart attack, and a compound fracture in his leg. He will not be gone long, he says. He takes the key and heads out for some fresh air in your new suburb, which he is visiting for the first time. While he is out, your wife and mother take your son and daughter for a walk to the park, which is close by. You are home waiting for your father and decide to run to the hardware store for some sandpaper for your son's pinewood-derby car. Without thinking, you set the alarm, like you do each time you leave the house. The house is empty.

Your father is the first to return from his outing. He unexpectedly beats you home. He unlocks the door and opens it. There is a high-pitched sound that fills the house, which sounds like his hearing aids when they are not adjusted correctly, which he does not hear because his hearing aids are turned down to their lowest setting to conserve money and energy. The alarm tone that he does not hear means that he has sixty seconds to enter the code, 1111, into the keypad, but he does not realize this because he cannot hear the high-pitched alarm tone. If the code is not entered within sixty seconds, the alarm will sound and the police will be notified; that's what the former owner told you, anyway.

Your father goes into the living room, sits down, and gets himself comfortable with the newspaper. Within five minutes, there are two police cars parked outside your house and the doorbell is ringing, the doorbell that your father cannot hear because he is saving money on his hearing-aid batteries. The police are knocking and ringing and their expressions are getting more serious as there continues to be no response. At that point, you pull up to your house with the sandpaper you purchased from the hardware store and see two police cars parked outside. One policeman is standing at your front door with his gun drawn and the other is crouched and trying to see into your living-room window.

You run to the front porch and ask the policeman what is wrong. The policeman tells you that the alarm has been triggered. He tells you that they are accustomed to false alarms—

"It happens all the time," he says—but usually people come to the door when that happens. You tell the two policemen to hold on, and you enter the house, because you think that your father may have something to do with the activated alarm. Inside the house, the alarm is sounding, a sound that you have never heard before. It is audible from the living room, where your father is sitting on the couch, reading the paper, like nothing is going on. He is really conserving his batteries now. You deactivate the alarm, go back outside, and tell the police that your father activated the alarm because he did not enter the code, and that he did not hear the alarm or the doorbell because he was saving money on his hearing-aid batteries. You thank the two officers for coming out and give each a doughnut, for which they are very appreciative.

You go back inside and your father looks up at you and says, "Is everything OK, my boy? I made it back to the house. Your neighbors look very nice."

Embrace Diversity

You live in a quaint and safe suburb with brick streets that seems as though it is 98.3 percent white and 1.7 percent Asian American. So 1.7 percent of the kids in your suburb will get better SAT scores than the other 98.3 percent. The only people of color that you have ever seen in your suburb are William Jones and the Jesse White Tumblers.

William Jones is a guy whom you brought into your suburb one Saturday morning for a kids' sports camp that you organize. Every Saturday morning in the summer, you meet fifteen to twenty kids, who are your kids' friends, along with their dads, who are your friends, and you play a sport. This Saturday, the kids will play football and you have invited William Jones to be the guest coach. You invited William because during your informational interview with him at work, as he was exploring different career options, you found out that he plays football for a college football team and he has a shot at the pros. You think that he is more qualified to teach your kids about football than anyone you know.

The Jesse White Tumblers are a group of African American kids, of all ages, who live in the projects in the city. They are world-class tumblers—fliers, you should really say. The team was started in 1959 by the current Illinois Secretary of State, Jesse White, who is also African American. The Jesse White Tumblers are so amazing that they perform all over the world. They are welcomed into your suburb one day a year, every Fourth of July, when they fly for your entire suburb.

Other than that, you see only white people like you 98.3 percent of the time, and 1.7 percent of the time, like when you go to the library, you see an occasional Asian American.

However, your suburb, before you moved into it, had chosen for itself—curiously—the slogan, "Unity Through Diversity." The emblem for your suburb's slogan, which you see affixed to many windshields, bumpers, and living-room windows, is a group of multiracial kids holding hands in a circle. The ethnicity shown in your suburb's emblem is more diverse than you have ever observed in your suburb since moving in.

You live by your suburb's slogan, but you are curious as to why your community selected this motto, over all others, to represent itself, given the homogeneity you observe. You conclude that it is easier to embrace "Unity Through Diversity" when there is none.

Find Religion

You are Catholic and your wife is Jewish. You barely discussed this with your wife before you got married, and it has never really been a topic of conversation since. You got married and it was not an issue. It is not an issue with your parents, who describe Judaism as one of the world's greatest religions.

Your wife's mother passes away sooner than she should have, and that is unfortunate. After that, your wife brings up the topic of having kids, which you have not really contemplated. You think that you are whole and that your life is good. You love your wife and you do what you can to make her happy. If she wants kids, then so do you. "Whatever will make you happy," you tell her.

So you get over that hurdle but then there is another. Your wife, all of a sudden, brings up the issue of religion, which has never been brought up before, except for maybe the time when you were dating and one day, sitting in her mother's kitchen, you asked her what happens to Jewish people when they die. She stammered and stuttered. It was the first time since you had met her that her quick wit and rapid-fire responses let her down. She did not know, and you thought that this was funny, because in your religion, the basic premise is that if you are bad you go to Hell, if you are good you go to Heaven, and if you are only OK you go to a holding tank called Purgatory. You think that, if nothing else, religion is intended to give you an understanding of the unknown, with the biggest unknown being death. You think that offering some vision of what happens when you die is the most fundamental premise of any religion, and about that, your wife had absolutely no clue.

You are clear about who you are and the religion that has given you your backbone. Your grandfather came to America from Italy. He met your Italian grandmother, whose family also immigrated from Italy. Your great-grandfather grew up and lived in a small town in Italy called Masse Lubrense and he built the town's only church, a spectacular church with a beautiful courtyard. You have twenty-five relatives in Italy and their heritage is rock solid. You know that your grandfather left his entire family to come to America to make a better life for his family. He learned a style of English that as a kid you never really understood, and he demanded that his children speak English because they were Americans now. In fact, your grandfather never even talked about being Italian until you were in high school or college and started to realize what was going on. You know that he worked fourteen- to sixteen-hour days in his own butcher shop to provide a better life for his kids and grandkids and that he instilled a work ethic that plagues you all, even today, with a need to be productive all the time.

You know that what gave him the courage and strength to do all this was his Catholic faith. You know your family's roots and you have no interest in abandoning them.

When your grandmother meets your wife-to-be for the first time, she asks, "So where is your family from?" You all know that when your grandmother asks this question what she means is what is your ethnicity. Your wife first answers, Olympia

Fields, Illinois, a suburb, which was meaningless to your grandmother, who believed that even Suffolk County, Long Island, was on another planet in the universe relative to her epicenter, Astoria, Queens, New York, where she lived. Your wife, who was your girlfriend at the time, soon realizes what your grandmother is asking, and after hesitating a moment, says that she is German. You all accept this and move on.

Ten years later you are in a room where someone else asks your wife that same question your grandmother posed ten years earlier, and your wife answers, "Russian." You are puzzled, because for the last decade you thought that she was German. You challenge her and she admits to you that she really does not know where she is from.

Rewind to when you were discussing kids and for the first time in the nine years since you have known your wife, religion becomes important to her. Not so much your religion, but the religion of the kids that your wife has been talking about having. She identifies Catholic and Jewish clergymen to assist in bringing clarity to this issue. The only problem is that after talking with the first religious professional, you understand that, in this instance, there is no compromise religion. She schedules one meeting after another, and to you this is a complete waste of time. To her, this is helping to clarify what has now surfaced as the most important issue in her life to resolve. You are puzzled as to why this has become such an urgent issue to your wife, who has never really focused on religious matters before.

Your wife's lack of understanding as to whether she is German or Russian or something else entirely, let alone her uncertainty as to what happens when you die, has made it difficult for you to understand your wife's passion to impart a religious heritage that she seems to know little about or have little connection with in any significant way to your children. You are puzzled why this

Jewish legacy is so important to your wife, but you do not probe in order to avoid conflict.

She lobbies with passion and wears you down to the point where you give in. You believe that a unified family is more important than anything and that nothing is significant enough to get in the way of that.

You agree that your children will be Jewish, and realize that you will always feel somewhat regretful that a part of your religious heritage that you know your grandfather worked so hard for and sacrificed so much for will be lost on your children. The deal you cut, though, includes celebrating all Catholic holidays, which to your delight have become your kids' favorites.

This is one way that your family will live out your suburban motto, "Unity Through Diversity."

YOUR SUBURBAN WORK-LIFE

Listen to Your Wife Ask Others for Advice

For ten years, you have been a corporate executive at The Merchandise Mart, the world's largest commercial building, which houses the world's most comprehensive collection of furniture showrooms. Among other things, The Merchandise Mart is a building full of office-furniture showrooms. It is the largest and most comprehensive collection of office furniture anywhere in the world. Once a year for the past thirty-five years, The Merchandise Mart has hosted the world's largest trade show for office furniture. In addition to the three hundred office-furniture companies that have showrooms at the Mart, another seven hundred companies come from all over the world to set up an exhibit space just for the show.

You run all the office-furniture–related business at The Merchandise Mart. This is one of the four business units you are responsible for running and the business that you have been involvd with the longest—for ten years. You are regarded as an international authority in this business, and you are quoted monthly in trade publications and the consumer press, even *The New York Times*, because they seek out your perspective for their readers. As a result of running this business, you know, personally, the presidents, owners, and sales and marketing vice presidents of just about every office-furniture company in the world. Because of what you do, you have played an instrumental role in helping many of these companies grow from small companies to medium-size companies and from medium-size companies to large companies. You have created more opportunities for these office-furniture companies to sell their chairs and desks than anyone in the entire history of this industry, and these companies, these business owners, presidents, and vice presidents, like you and respect you because of it. They treat you well when they see you, and they seek out your opinions, ideas, and direction. Many would appreciate the opportunity to do you a favor. Whenever you need a furniture-related favor, you can ask one of a thousand people and they will accommodate you. You have gotten furniture for many people, including many of your friend-boss's family. They know that you are the go-to guy when it comes to anything to do with office furniture.

You come home one day and walk into your house. Your wife is on the phone with one of her friends and she is talking about office chairs. She is writing down all of the specifications of the chair that her friend has bought. Your wife gets off the phone and tells you that you need two more office chairs for your home office. Now that the kids' bathroom ceiling is the right color, it is time to focus on getting the home office set up just right. Your wife then shows you a catalogue page from Office Resources, an office-supply superstore, for the chairs that she would like to get for the office, the one her friend has told her is so good. You know that the chairs from Office Resources are the lowest-quality chairs that you can get. You look at her in amazement. "Honey, do you understand what I have been doing after leaving the house every morning for the past ten years when I go to work? Do you understand the business that I run and that I know just about every chair in the market and have met the designers who designed them and the company owners who brought them to market?"

You remind her that if she has any questions about office furniture she may consider consulting with you. She says that she would, but that her friend Jane, a stay-at-home mom, whose entire exposure to the office-furniture industry consists of her one brief visit to Office Resources, says that she got the best chair from Office Resources and it was only $100. You tell her that you will take care of it. "What kind of chairs will you get?" she asks. "Good ones," you say.

Four days later, you arrive home with two Aeron chairs, which of course you got at an amazing discount. They have been recognized as one of the best chairs on the market for the past nine years. Your friend, a top executive of the company that makes Aeron chairs, was happy to help you out. Excitedly, you take the chairs upstairs and position them in your office. Now you have three chairs in your home office. There, perfect, you think, so much better than those Office Resources chairs your wife's friend was talking about. Your wife looks at you and says, "I think that we have too many chairs in here."

Go to Work

In the suburb that you live in, people pretty much do four things to earn money to support their families and their lifestyles:

1. They are top corporate executives.
2. They are doctors or lawyers.
3. They are successful entrepreneurs who own their own businesses.
4. They are retired, having cashed out of something.

Your fortunate neighbors who are in this fourth category of "worker" really get you pissed off. While you all aspire to be the guy in that No. 4 category, unless you are there you really don't want to hear about it. It is difficult for you to feel good about people who have landed in category No. 4, because they have something that you do not have, but want.

Just the other day, your wife was standing at the bus stop with three other moms, waiting for the bus with the kids. Dean, for the first time ever in his life, shows up at the bus stop with his kid. "Oh, Dean, are you off today?" another mom,

Susan, asks, your wife relates to you that night after you come home. "No," he says, "I have just cashed out of a company that I brought public and will be getting an enormous sum of money in two months." He goes on, not noticing the look of disgust in each of the moms' expressions, "I am retired!"

That was Dean's way of breaking his big news to his neighbors, all of whom would never admit that they wanted to emulate Dean but who, in the meantime, until they achieved his position in life, would scorn him. "Who would want to retire?" all of the husbands respond to their wives, who have been waiting all day to break the big news to all of you.

"We love our work, and seeing us work provides a good value structure for the kids," you say in unison at your separate dinner tables, trying to justify your nine-to-five suburban existence with some degree of dignity.

When you first move into this suburb from the city, you think that you are a real big shot. You have a big-time job and see yourself as a big-time corporate executive.

Further, you think you are a real big shot because you played a role in increasing the value of the world's largest commercial building and you were rewarded for it. From that, your own real-estate investments, and your investment income, you are pulling down some real didge. You, my man, are in the top 1 percent. You have been able to buy a house in one of the country's most expensive suburbs and have the luxury of staying in your old city house for eight months until your renovations are done and then moving in to your new home when you feel like it. Shortly after moving in, you are able to upgrade to epoxy grout and buy new towels that match it (but that do not dry you), and pay $1,600 to change the color of the kids' bathroom ceiling, which no one will ever see. You have arrived.

You buy the house and for the price you pay you think that

you should be living on some big parcel of land, an estate, on a hill overlooking the lake, and that your house should ramble, with rooms that you don't even know what to call. You are not, it does not, and anyone would call each room in your house the same thing that you call each room in your house.

Slowly, you come to realize that you are not the big shot you thought you were. You live in a suburb where everyone is at least as big a shot as you are, and many are much bigger shots. You never realized that there were so many opportunities to be a bigger shot than you. You are invited to houses that *do* ramble and that *do* overlook the lake. You know what you paid for your house, and you think that if you added perhaps a zero you would be close to approximating the values of many of the houses you are invited into.

You know what you do and what you pull down to live where you live, and you sometimes have a hard time imagining what so-and-so does or did to live in a house that your five-year-old daughter would describe as "ginormous" and that your son would describe as "scaled up from what we have." As in "Daddy, why is it that everything the [numerous people] have is scaled up from what we have?" a question that you avoid answering. "Their climbing wall is higher, their zip line is longer, their house is taller, their yard is bigger, and they have a built-in pool that does not have to be emptied each night and put back in the garage."

On a Friday, you come home from work, fighting the battles that a corporate executive fights on a typical Friday, and your then eight-year-old son asks, "Dad, why do you have to go to work? Can't you stay home like Paul's dad or like Eric's dad or like John's dad?"—three of the kids' dads that he happened to see while playing that day. You try to think of a reply that will resonate with your kid to reinforce a strong work ethic in him, like the one that you grew up with, but it is difficult without degrading the other dads, whom you secretly aspire to be like.

You think of something clever and you say, without admitting that for the time being these guys are beating you in this competition, "You know, son, those dads may be home every day, but my guess is that I probably spend as much time with you and your sister as those dads do with their kids." You say this having no clue as to how much time any of these dads spend with their kids. Your kid thinks about what you have said and looks at you and nods his head in agreement.

Go Buy Some Wholesale Suits

The only thing that you like better than wholesale is free. Every day, you wear a suit to work; that is the culture where you work, in contrast to Dean, who by now has probably received his "enormous sum of money" and whose new "work" uniform is a pair of shorts, a T-shirt, and sandals.

There is nothing about shopping that you enjoy, so the last time you bought suits was a few years ago. You bought ten. Now many of these suits are wearing out. You are not like your father in this regard. He would have a rotation pattern with his suits, where he would retire two suits each year and replace them with two new ones.

You go for the one-shot big buy, and this is no problem for you because you think you are a big-shot corporate executive. For a few months, the fact that you need some new suits has been rolling around in the back of your mind and then, for two reasons, you decide to act. First, this thought surfaces more and more often, like when you are visiting with the president of the largest furniture company in the world and you take your jacket off to reveal a tear in the lining that is large enough to place a copy of this book into. Second, you have been seeing advertisements for a place that sells wholesale suits, aptly named Wholesale Suits, which sells to consumers one day a week.

You call this place and they tell you that they have brand-name suits, not seconds or anything like that. The suits are three for the price of one. The man tells you that there are a lot of Italian suits, which draws you in, and that you can get *three* suits for either $300, $400, $500, $600, or $700, depending on the quality. The price is right.

You call back and ask for directions, because the map they have provided is of no help to you. There is not one recognizable road or highway on it. You get the directions and realize that you are committing yourself to at least a forty-five-minute drive to get there, assuming you do not get lost, which you will. You must shop on a Saturday, consumer day, and you hate to do anything that takes you away from your family on what you have established as family day.

You go one day when your kids both have playdates. You drive on roads that you have never seen before, and after one hour and fifteen minutes you pull up to an unmarked warehouse. The parking lot is nearly full. The man that you talked to on the phone was right. This windowless, one-story box of a warehouse is chock-full of suits, and the prices are what he told you they would be, cheap.

You go to the 40-regular section and have a man that you think works there point out the area for three-button suits, because you think they are in style now. In about five minutes you pull off fifteen that look good to you and begin trying them on. Like eating and showering, shopping is something that you like to do fast. Ten of the fifteen fit, and you buy them. You spend $2,000 for these suits, $200 each, and, to you, each one looks like a $1,000 suit. You are smart! You notice some labels that you think you recognize, like Armani and DKNY; that is good, right?

You confirm with the checkout guy that these are not rejects and he assures you that they are not. First quality, you think he says, in a difficult-to-understand Eastern European accent. You do not have these suits altered there, because you know that having to pick them up will mean another drive out to this nameless suburb with loud airplanes flying overhead every forty-five seconds.

You take the suits home and proudly show the big pile to your family. They feign interest for a minute or so and then go back to whatever they were doing. You call a tailor that you find in the phone book, the one closest to your home, and ask if he can alter ten suits for you. He thinks that you are joking. "Nobody buys ten suits," he says. "I will see you in five minutes," you say. You show up and you tell the tailor what a terrific deal you got on the suits. By doing this, you want to prove to him that you are a smart guy and not the obnoxious spoiled brat that he thinks you are, showing up with ten new suits to tailor.

He marks one suit and says he will alter all the other ones to match. This is perfect. You do not waste any more time than you have to on this taking-you-away-from-your-family chore.

You pick up the suits on Wednesday after work and pay the tailor $113, and he seems much less impressed with your purchases today than when you brought them in on Saturday. He does not treat you like the big shot that he thought you were then.

On Thursday, you select one of your new suits and wear it to work. You feel good, like a man wearing a new suit should feel, all day long. As you are driving home, you feel a more pronounced breeze on your right leg than usual, and when you look down at your leg you see it—your leg, that is. The seam has separated on the outside of your leg from your hip to your knee on this day when you christened your new suit. You are unsure how long this condition has existed, but you suspect that your colleagues have a much more accurate sense of when this situation transpired. You give them the benefit of the doubt by assuming that they were just too polite to tell you.

You stop off at the tailor on your way home that evening and he "reinforces" your pant leg while you stand in the dressing room in your underwear. He asks again how much you paid for your suit. You respond, "Not enough."

On your way out, he says, "See you soon." He is right.

Take the Train to Work

One sure way to tell if you live in the suburbs or not is by the seats in the train that stops somewhere near where you live. If the train seats are hard-surfaced, molded plastic, or have only a quarter inch or so of inadequate padding, with the seat backs at something close to a ninety-degree angle, then you *do not* live in a suburb. You live in the city.

However, if the train that stops near where you live has four- or five-inch-thick leather-covered padding on the seats and seat backs, and if the seat backs are at a more comfortable angle—say, seventy-five degrees—and if you can rotate the seat backs so that you can reconfigure the train seats to oppose one another, then you live in the suburbs.

When you take a train from the suburbs, you usually take it to the city. It is one way corporate executives get to and from work every Monday through Friday. There is great similarity in the way people who take the train that you take are dressed. Even in this day and age of casual dress, most men on the train that you take into work wear dark suits, white shirts, maroon ties (usually), and shiny black shoes. Each suit-wearing person on that train platform, you assume, has paid more for their suit than you have for yours, and each has most definitely visited his tailor less frequently than you have yours. They usually carry a briefcase.

Women are usually very well dressed. They wear what you think they call pantsuits and they wear professional-looking skirt suits. They wear shoes with heels that are not too high, so as not to give the wrong impression to other corporate executives. They, too, carry something you might call a briefcase.

On the train that you take, these uniforms are worn by just about all of your fellow commuters, with one very significant exception. There is one person whom you take note of because "she" is a unique-looking individual. To you, it looks as though "she" would fit in better if "she" were sitting on a train with the hard-shelled, plastic molded seats with little or no padding.

There are a few things that give you this impression. "Her" physical characteristics are as follows:

"She":

has long thick blond flowing hair that is waist-length;
is slender;
has long legs;
wears tight, usually black stretch pants that flare at the bottom;
wears a tight, collared black knit shirt with a minimum of three buttons open;
wears high-heeled shoes, accentuating an unusually tall frame;
accessorizes with two-inch-diameter hoop earrings;
has cleavage like a female weight lifter;
has long fingernails that are manicured;
wears very tight black leather gloves when it is cold out;
walks with a great deal of confidence;

has a runway-trained cadence;

from the back, looks like the most attractive woman on the platform;

is allocated more personal space than all other passengers;

is usually the only person who has a seat all by "herself" all the way into the city;

has visible panty lines;

wears black eyeliner;

sits on the train with "her" thighs pressed very closely together;

has a clean-shaven face;

has an Adam's apple.

What is interesting is that this individual has selected to live either in your suburb or the suburb that is immediately south of yours. "She" has chosen to live in an area that everyone else has chosen because there are good schools for the kids and plenty of kids to play with. You hope that "she" has chosen this area to live for other reasons.

You, like everyone else on this train, wonder where this person lives, where "she" works, and why "she" dresses like "she" does—questions that will remain unanswered, because knowing the answers to these questions would require talking to this person, something that nobody on this train has been willing to attempt in the past four years.

Support Your Wife in Her Pursuit of Making Money

Your wife, like many wives in your suburb, is well educated.

Your wife is now a full-fledged stay-at-home mom. The kids are now in school and, having a desire to do something professionally and few mental roadblocks, your wife gets the idea that she is a clothing designer and begins designing clothing for kids. She names the company after your children, whose names become an acronym for a lengthy company name that you can never remember exactly. She designs kids' and women's sweaters and skirts. They are knit and they have chenille, you have heard her say repeatedly.

Her sweaters are cool and everyone who sees them likes them. She finds a woman in a run-down neighborhood who lives in a small, run-down two-unit apartment building who has some friends that have knitting machines, which to you look a little like electronic keyboards. These women, in the unfinished and unheated basement of this two-flat, become your wife's "factory," as she likes to describe it.

They while away the hours and make sweater after sweater to fill order after order.

The sweaters do look great, and wherever you go people are

talking about this new apparel line. Sometimes you go places and people are wearing her clothes, which they have purchased at Barneys, Nordstrom's, or some high-end boutique on Armitage Street in the city or in SoHo. The sweaters are not cheap either. You don't really remember, but a kid's sweater would sell for something like $200. You and your wife cannot really believe that there are people who buy $200 sweaters for their kids, and you laugh about the absurdity of this. But, hey, they do.

On occasion, you ask your wife if she is keeping track of her revenues and expenses. She responds, "Keeping track of what?" You try to assist her in creating a simple-to-use spreadsheet that will help her (and you, as the de-facto venture capitalist in this new venture) determine if she is making any money selling these $200 sweaters. This is not your wife's forte. She gets frustrated with you every time you bring this up, because she is a *designer*. She cannot be bothered with the non-creative aspects of this one-person business.

You try several times to understand the material and labor costs and how they relate to the price that she sells the sweaters for, because Brian, your ex-accountant, who is probably checking in a naked couple right now, is no longer available to probe these issues for you. Your wife tries to help you with these numbers but mostly looks at you with a blank expression and then adorably admits that she has no idea. "I am a *designer*," she says.

For two years, you try to assist the *designer* you married to understand the financial impact of what she is doing so that you can understand the financial impact of your investment in this venture, which requires frequent cash calls. She gets frustrated. She spends a lot of time driving to her "factory," which is located in a neighborhood where gang graffiti decorates most of the homes and where sneakers are draped over telephone wires.

There is always a big pile of sweaters in your SUV and you have to build a storage room in your 1920s suburban house that acts as the "warehouse" for mounds of $200 kids' sweaters. You add the cost of your new warehouse to the capital-expense line item on the income statement that you are trying to assemble with little help from your wife. The good news is that for two years you have no taxes to pay on the business that shares a name with your kids. Your new accountant, who has a wife you have met, offers no comment on this development.

Barneys files for bankruptcy and the reps don't feel like pioneering this new line. The only way that this business will take off is if your wife devotes all of her time to it. She chooses not to and has a sample sale to sell off the inventory in your "warehouse." You will not be looking forward to an enormous sum of money coming from this business anytime soon.

YOUR
SUBURBAN
FRIENDS AND
NEIGHBORS

Meet Your Loving Neighbor

Your neighbors are very friendly, which is something that you really like about your suburb. A few, however, are maybe too friendly. David Golob falls into that category. He tells you that he loves you, and he tells you this each time that he sees you. And you think that he makes it a point to see you often so that he can maximize the number of times that he tells you that he loves you. In the city you didn't have any neighbors who told you that they loved you, and you appreciated that about the city. In fact, you did not even know most of your neighbors in the city.

At first you think that maybe this is the way neighbors express themselves to one another in the suburbs, and that concerns you. This is not the kind of "Unity Through Diversity" that you signed on for when you moved to the suburbs.

Now, if this were your neighbor across the street, Annika, expressing such thoughts, it would probably be something with which you could deal a little better. Annika is the kind of "Unity Through Diversity" that you can handle any day of the week. But this is David Golob, and while you believe he is one of the most sincere guys around, you have five problems with him telling you that he loves you each time he sees you:

1. David is a man, and when any man repeats these three words to you it makes you extremely uncomfortable.
2. David is probably ten years your senior.
3. David is married with children and lives in the house behind yours.
4. David shares an alley with you.
5. David seems to time his comings and goings around yours.

David "runs into" you frequently as you are opening your garage door to pull out of your garage. You imagine that he spends a lot of his time watching your rear door to see when you leave so that he can leave his house at the same time and "accidentally" run into you in the alley. You think that he does this so that he can tell you he loves you and tell you that you are the salt of the earth each time he "coincidentally" runs into you in the alley.

You begin developing fake-out tactics to avoid his words of affection. One tactic involves exiting the rear door of your house and then stalling before entering your detached garage, hoping that David will have left before you open your garage door. Only it doesn't work. You think that somehow, unknowingly, you have struck a special chord in David and that for some reason he has singled you out as the neighbor onto whom he will shed his love. You soon learn differently.

When David sees your wife, he says that he loves her too. "You and Mark are the salt of the earth," he says, immediately after telling your wife that he loves her. You are not quite exactly sure what that expression means but you are positive that you have about as much comfort with David telling your wife that he loves her as you do with him telling you that he loves you, which is none. All this talk of love makes you nervous about your new neighbor.

After this you become more curious about David and begin making inquiries about his loving behavior. You soon learn that David loves many of your neighbors including Peter, Bonnie, Robert, Margo, Jamie, Mary, Ellen, Paul, Eddie, and Bernie and that they too are the salt of the earth. They have all accepted David's outpouring of affection as "That's just David." While you hope that you never get comfortable with all this talk of love and salt, and you will do your best to avoid it, you conclude that this is just David's way of being a good suburban neighbor.

Go to a Dinner Party

Your wife takes care of your social calendar, and for this you are mostly thankful. She knows a lot of different people and always has something interesting arranged. She is a social animal and the unofficial mayor of your suburb. She believes, as she should, that she is in command of your social schedule, and generally you are thankful for this. You know a lot of people because of your wife, you go to a lot of parties because of your wife, and you see some good movies because of your wife and some others that you can live without, like *Fried Green Tomatoes*. For the most part, this unspoken arrangement works to your advantage, with two minor exceptions.

First, in this arrangement, you can never schedule any social function on your own. This is a mistake. Your wife will have already committed you to be somewhere else. She will get angry at you because you have taken the initiative to make your own social choice, an activity in which she engages all the time. This is her turf; do not encroach on it. If you do make some plan, it is not what your wife would like to do. The time is wrong because your daughter has to nap then and your son will be hungry. You will schedule something over one of your kids' friends' birthday parties or a sleepover. The location will be wrong. "What? We have to drive there?" your wife will ask accusingly. "Why can't they come here?" And/or the people will be wrong, mostly because they are your friends and not really hers.

The second downside of this arrangement is the fact that your wife, if you are lucky, will give you up to one hour's prior notice before any particular social function that she has arranged for you. Usually it's a half hour. You deal with this fine. You are a man with flow. You are flexible and adaptable. You are ready for anything. You roll with it.

Generally, you have no issues with this arrangement except when your wife gets angry at you for not being ready for an event that you have absolutely no idea that you are attending.

For example, one Friday evening you come home from one hell of a week. You eat a light dinner with your family, hang out with your kids, and before you know it, it's their bedtime. On this night, your wife puts your daughter to bed, and you do the same with your son. You read with him (he reads his book and you yours), you turn out the lights, you tell him a story, and then the two of you say a prayer (a Catholic one). This has become your nightly routine and you both like it. Your job is done and you go to your bedroom. You are engaged in a book called *The Gold Coast*, by Nelson DeMille, and you want to read it now. You go into your closet, put on your pajamas, go to the bathroom and brush your teeth, wash your face and try to dry it with your herringbone-patterned towel, and slip into bed and begin reading. Your face is damp.

A few minutes later, your wife comes upstairs and she looks at you in disbelief. She is startled and angry. "What are you doing?" she asks. You respond that you are lying in bed and that you are reading the book that you have been enjoying. It is a book about an Italian mob guy who moves into a Waspy old-money Long Island town called Old Westbury.

She looks at you, demanding a response to her next question, "Why aren't you ready? You have been up here all this time and you are not ready? We are late. The babysitter is downstairs." You did not hear anyone enter your house. "Babysitter? Late for what? Where are we going?" you ask. "Where are we going?" your wife responds. "We are going to the Fairchilds'. They are having a dinner party and we are late. It has been on my calendar for a month! Get ready."

This is the first time you have heard of any dinner-party plans, but this does not surprise you. You say, "Oh, OK." You get out of bed, get dressed, and head downstairs. You greet the babysitter and you inform her that you are going to the Fairchilds' for a dinner party. She tells you that she knows that because your wife told her three weeks ago.

You wait for your wife, another activity to which you have grown accustomed. You wait some more. Fifteen minutes later, you begin walking to the Fairchilds' for the second dinner that you will eat that evening.

Be Deprived of Your Favorite Beverage

You love fruit juices without sweetener, and purple grape juice is your very favorite, especially when mixed with sparkling water.

After your first child was born, your wife ceased to buy grape juice for you. She never explains her rationale for this move and she never notifies you of this development. You just notice it after awhile and then you sort of forget about it. What you do realize about this development is that, for whatever reason, your wife does not want grape juice in the house, and you respect her wish.

You cannot think of any logical reason why your wife has pursued this course of action, but you assume her logic may flow something like this. She may be concerned that if the baby sees you drinking grape juice then he may want some, too, and if he has some he might spill it. If he spills it, he may make a mess and stain something. This is one possible explanation that you have thought of for why your wife does not buy you grape juice anymore.

The other possibility that you think of, which is a little more abstract but more in line with how your wife thinks, is that life, for your wife, with a baby, is now more work. She has less control over her time. In her mind, she has less time to do things that are for her own enjoyment because she has a baby to take care of. In order for you to share that pain with her, she will deprive you of things that she knows you enjoy, simple things in life, starting with grape juice at home. You think that she will feel better knowing that you are deprived of the things you like. Unfortunately, this principle does not apply to the things that you wish your wife would *stop* buying, like new towels. Rather, her theory will apply only to the things that you enjoy most in life, like purple grape juice and sex.

You have the next seven years to dwell on this, because it is that long since you have had grape juice at home. One day, after seven years of grape-juice deprivation and a day after your dinner at the Fairchilds', you see a new sight in your refrigerator: a pitcher of grape juice. You wonder what has prompted your wife's first purchase of this delightful beverage after this seven-year hiatus. Then you recall a conversation that you had when you were over for dinner at the Fairchilds'.

That evening, you and your friends had a funny conversation about things that your wives deprive you of, things that you really enjoy. The story about grape juice surfaces, although it is not the first example that is brought up to illustrate this phenomenon. Because of this conversation, for the first time in seven years your wife may have realized how irrational her logic was. That is unlikely.

More likely, you suspect, is that after you tell this grape-juice story your friend's wife said to your wife, but not in front of you, "He is such a nice guy, a great husband, an involved father, a talented coach, and he builds a mean pinewood-derby car. Why don't you just go out and buy the guy some grape juice? It is so much easier than having sex."

The next day, you come home and there is a pitcher of grape juice waiting for you in the refrigerator. You do not have sex that night.

Have an Affair

You shouldn't really even be writing this story, because you don't know the people involved, you have never met them, nor do you know any of the facts. The reason that you know so much about this story is that for about a year and a half or so, at every single social event that you attend, a story about a woman—let's call her Christine—and a guy you will refer to as her golf instructor, would work its way into every conversation. It is an unusual story, because your suburb is very stable. You do not know any individual who lives in your suburb who has had an affair. You have never had an affair. You think that if this type of thing is going on then it is not talked about, but more than likely it simply does not occur. With one exception.

For a year and a half you have listened to story after story about a woman you have never met, have never (to your knowledge) seen, and don't even know by name. You listened silently to each and every one of these stories. Christine has been married for many years and has three young elementary-school-aged children. She would take golf lessons, in a foursome, with three other women, all around forty or forty-five years old. Each week, year-round, Christine and her friends would meet with their golf instructor, François, each Tuesday at 10 A.M.

Christine and her friends would meet with François when her husband—let's call him Bob—was at the office being an accountant, tallying columns of numbers, wishing that he owned a nudist hotel in Southern California or Palm something or other, or whatever it is that accountants do, making a living to pay the mortgage on his overpriced home and to allow his wife the freedom to stay at home with the kids and do things like take golf lessons during the day.

Christine's golf teacher, François, is French. At age eighteen, he is still a boy in many respects, and he still lives at home with his parents. François forked over an extra $15 to get custom license plates that read GOLFPRO, which is how François likes to think of himself.

While Christine is taking golf lessons from François with her three friends, she starts liking the part of the lesson where François would reach around her from behind to adjust her grip on the shaft of her driver. Before long, Christine would feel a little moisture between her legs when François came to this part of the lesson. François, noticing a more relaxed expression on Christine when he reached around her, would spend a little more time with her to offer some additional instruction on how firm her grip should be and exactly where her hands should be placed on the shaft of the club to maximize the power in her stroke. François, a very diligent instructor, would make sure Christine started out with the proper grip, which required frequent adjustment throughout the lesson.

Christine's fellow students started noticing the extra attention that Christine was getting, and enjoying, from François. Before long, Christine's friends booked François for a different time, leaving Christine to go one on one with François, which, as you have heard, they did frequently. Pretty soon, Christine's neighbors began to notice a car parked outside Christine's house at various times, but always after the kids went to school and before they returned home, with license plates that read GOLFPRO. Suspicions were raised, because many people—particularly women—take golf lessons from François and know his famous plates. There was much talk among people in your suburb about this marked car outside Christine's house. Your neighbors had heard the stories that were circulating and started to put one and one together.

One day, Christine's son came home from first grade and asked his mother why his friends were telling him that his mommy had a boyfriend who played golf. François even showed up at a holiday party that Christine and her husband, Bob, threw at their house. You heard, from those who were in attendance, that Christine paid an inordinate amount of attention to François that night, making many of her guests uncomfortable. Most left early, out of respect for Bob, because they did not want Bob to think that they were condoning Christine's behavior.

This story has no good ending for anyone.

Watch Your Neighbors Move

You live in an upwardly mobile suburb. You can say this because there is evidence all around you. You witness your neighbors buy one house, then trade up to another house just a few blocks away. You observe this house-flipping and you hear about it occasionally because it is the talk at the cocktail parties that you go to. You think that this activity of frequent house-flipping may be disruptive to a family, and these frequent conversations do not really draw you in.

One day, however, you meet a genuine house-flipper who could write a book on the topic. You meet people who, while it does not appear to be their mission, have sort of assumed house-flipping as a lifestyle. It is not what you would call an intentional activity for these people, more an involuntary activity, where you move and, just as you are settled, you move again. Like other involuntary activities, if you don't move you will be uncomfortable, and when you move you are not so aware of what you are doing.

Like most of the people you have met, you meet the movers through your wife. Your wife becomes friends with your kid's buddy Paul Schiller's mom. And, because your kid's friend's mom has become your wife's friend, then you, being at the tail end of this food chain, will become friends with your kid's friend's dad. When you meet these people, you would not have guessed them to be house-flippers, but they are.

You first meet the Schiller family when they are 90 percent completed with the renovation of their home. Because you did not know the home before they poured and poured money into it, your frame of reference is what you are told. You have had these discussions many times. People will draw imaginary lines in the air to tell you where old homes ended and new additions begin. They will gesture with two outstretched palms to describe to you where the stairway once was and will point out rooms that are now kitchens and studies that were once living rooms and bedrooms. You feign interest during these house tours but are really hoping that some kid will fall and scream so that you will have a legitimate excuse to break away.

You know a few of what you would call top-line issues regarding this house renovation. First of all, there were hundreds and hundreds of thousands of dollars in change orders. A change order is when you plan to do one thing when you only have drawings, and your contractor gives you a price on that, and then, when you see the home under construction, you have a different idea about what it should look like, resulting in changes and thus, change orders. As you go through this house tour, you hear of one midstream change order after another. These are the changes that a contractor loves, because he knows that he has you. Predictably, a contractor will tell you that the architect should have thought of that earlier, and that in order to do it right it will cost you tens of thousands of dollars more, first to undo what has been done and then to do what will make you happy. Contractors make their money on change orders. The other thing that you conclude about this project is that the addition doubled the size of the preexisting house. There are rooms in this house that even the Schillers do not know what to call or how to use. In this renovation, you have no question that wherever there is grout it is epoxy grout.

After two years, the project is almost complete and your new friends tell you how much of a living hell the last two years of their life have been. They were quarantined in one section of the house while the contractor took over another. They had one temporary kitchen set up in the dining room before it was moved to the living room. Dishes were washed each night in a small bathroom sink. In the middle of all of this they had a baby. Every day, there are at least five contractors in the house, all day long.

They are happy now that the house is 90 percent done. Fireplace surrounds, molding, and things like that are the only things remaining to be completed.

Two months later, you go to the Schillers' house to pick up Paul to take him and your son to a big field to shoot off rockets. As you pull up to the house, you notice a For Sale sign outside. You walk up to the front door and tell your new friend jokingly that someone stuck a For Sale sign on his front lawn. "We're selling," he announces to you. "I'm a trader," he states, "and we are ready to trade." You are astonished.

Two months later, the house is sold for a record price on this pricey block in this pricey suburb. The Schillers have to move out in forty-five days. You notice the sale price of $2.25 million in your suburban paper, which reports all sales, but after hearing about all those change orders you are not so sure that your friends made money on this trade. You do not ask them to confirm your impression.

They move into a rental in the part of your suburb where you live, close to the school, the lake, and their former home. It is, at a minimum, a $10,000-per-month proposition. Your new friends decide to settle for a while in this rental while they find something suitable for themselves to buy. They are planning to rent for only a month or two, you are told, but they move their furniture, clothes, toys, sporting equipment, trampoline, bikes, stereos, tableware, TVs, and everything else to the rental and unpack all of it. They want to get their five kids situated in the manner to which they have grown accustomed.

Four months into the rental, they find the perfect house to buy. It is a house that they will spend $1 million on and it is on a corner lot, like their last home. But there is no way that these new friends of yours can live in that million-dollar house the way it is. It is not suitable, it needs a "ton of work." They hire an architect, who you guess will charge somewhere around $60,000 to $80,000 to work up a set of drawings and to obtain permits. The architect takes four months to develop these plans. You do the math: architect's fees plus monthly rental plus principal and interest on an $800,000 loan. You figure that without any architect's fees or other incidentals this transition is costing your friends $17,000 to $20,000 per month.

Because your other friends know that the Schillers are your friends, you field a lot of questions about what these people are doing. "Why don't they move into their new house?" your other friends ask. "Isn't that house good enough for them?" they ask. You respond that you are not so sure what they are doing, and that you think they may not be so sure, either.

After all that, work never begins on the new million-dollar house; it sits vacant for another six months. Two months later, you see a For Sale sign posted on the lawn of this never-lived-in house. "We are moving to Chappaqua," your new friends announce to your wife. "We are going out looking for homes this week. Jeff got a new job."

They come back and Jill calls your wife. They have found a house, but it needs so much work, she tells your wife. "It is a small house," she says. Of course it does and of course it is, your wife responds. Two months later your friends pack up and move.

Six months later, you see in the paper, confirming what you

suspected, that the house that your new friends acquired but never moved into has been sold for $200,000 less than what your new friends paid for it. The Fairchilds bought it.

Three months later, just after the Chappaqua house renovation has wound down, your wife gets a call from Jill. "We are moving back," she says. "We found a house, but it needs a ton of work."

YOUR SUBURBAN WINTER

Send and Receive Holiday Cards

It is the holiday season. Your earliest recollections of the holiday season include the exchanging of Christmas cards among friends and family. You remember your mother and father keeping track of who sent them holiday cards when you were a young child. But, like most people, you assume, they also kept track of who *did not* send them a holiday card. The people on this list were delegated to friendship purgatory, so to speak, unless they had a death in the family, in which case they were legitimately excused from sending a holiday card that year. This was an important mental list, and so you grew up thinking that there were very few things that were more important than sending holiday cards to your friends and family during the holiday season. Sending holiday cards is a genetic impulse that has been passed along to you.

It's December 5, and you ask your wife, "Honey, do we have a holiday card yet?" assuming that she has taken care of this detail that, although you have never spoken about it, is a job that you believe to be hers. You are hoping for an answer of yes, but your hopes soon fade.

As she does every year at this time, she looks at you and asks,

"Do we really need to send out a holiday card this year?" You imagine everyone you know walking around with their mental checklist, this blacklist that your parents maintained, and you respond as follows: "What are you talking about? Of course we have to send out a holiday card. It's the holiday season. What can you possibly be thinking?" Reluctantly, she acknowledges that you are right, a rare admission. "What are we going to send out?" she asks. "I don't know," you respond, but you have noticed since moving to your suburb that every single card you get includes a photograph of kids or of entire families. Each one is elaborate and there is no money spared on these once-a-year greetings. One guy you know, who does not have a wife or kids, sends out a card with a photo of his dog, Bart, on it. "Whatever we do, the card has to have a photo," you say to your wife.

You think back to when you were growing up. Most of the cards you received were generic and were simply purchased at a store. The majority of them had a stylized green Christmas tree on the front or some quaint, snow-covered scene. Out of the big stack of cards that came in, only one or two came with photos, and those were always from the people who lived in the largest houses that you had been to, in suburbs that were different from your own.

You think about it and realize that there has been a cultural shift in card-giving, or, come to think of it, maybe you shifted cultures; you are not so sure which. Now you cannot send or receive a card that does not include a family photo, usually taken in some exotic locale. As if that is not enough, the exact location is usually graphically typeset in a not-to-be-missed place on the card.

You enjoy sending out funny cards, and you want to come up with something better than the Halloween-themed Christmas card that your wife selected last year. You thought that it was odd to send out a Christmas card with a photo of your son as Frankenstein and your daughter as a fairy princess on it, and, judging from the lack of comments from your friends and family, they did, too. But the reality is that when your wife showed you the Halloween photo that she selected and thought to be the best kid photo out of the five hundred or so pictures that you had of them that year, you rejected it outright when she asked for your opinion. You told her that you thought it was inappropriate to send out a Christmas card with a photo of your kids dressed for Halloween, and suggested that if she wanted your friends and family to see that photo perhaps you could send out a Halloween card next October. This opinion, which you offered to your wife upon her request, like many opinions that you offer, did not matter to her. She liked that Halloween picture and that was the only good photo that you had of the kids, according to her.

That year, while you were awaiting your wife's idea for the card and for the photo, you noticed a shoe box in the dining room. "What's that?" you asked your wife, noting that it was unusual for there to be a shoe box in the dining room. "The Christmas cards," she responded. "That what?" You opened the box to see three hundred cards, all of which have a photo of your son as Frankenstein and your daughter as the fairy princess on the front. You couldn't quite believe that this would be sent to your closest three hundred friends and family members, including your parents, Brian and his "wife" at the Clayton Inn, the Fairchilds, Annika, and your friend-boss and his family, who you are sure would all react like you, thinking, "Why did the Falangas send out a Halloween photo for Christmas? What were they thinking?" This is bad, you thought. You ignored it and made a mental note to assert yourself more next year. You received not even one single follow-up complimentary call on your card that year. Of the hundreds of cards you received, there were none that were Halloween-themed, like yours.

This year, you are more engaged in the process. You would

like something funny, but neither you nor your wife has an idea. Nothing clever comes to mind, and you feel that you have to do something big to make up for last year. You put your wife up to the challenge. "What kind of funny Christmas card can we come up with this year?" you ask. You both think on it and think on it some more and cannot come up with anything.

Then your wife, who seems to have hundreds of friends with whom she confers on even the most mundane aspects of her life, calls Karen, her most creative friend in matters of graphic design, to see if she has any ideas.

Not even an hour later, Karen calls back, while she is clearing the dinner table, and tells your wife that she has an idea. In less than one hour, while she was preparing dinner and feeding her three kids, Karen, who has never celebrated Christmas in her entire life, calls your wife and reveals her idea for your card. "How about 'Happy Holidays from the Falalalalalalalangas,'" she says.

Instantly, you and your wife know that there will never be any holiday card from the Falangas better than that. You have had the last name Falanga for your entire life, and your wife has had it for fifteen years. No one, in generations of Falangas, has ever thought of this idea—not your parents, grandparents, great-grandparents, or anyone before them. No other relatives, either. Karen, who has never celebrated Christmas, did in less than an hour what the Falangas have not done in at least four generations.

Your wife finds a printer and she takes Karen's unbelievable concept to him and in three days you have what you know will be *the* big-hit holiday card in your suburb. You will more than make up for last year with this card and you have Karen to thank. The cards go out and the calls pour in.

Prove to Your Kids That There Really Is a Santa

Your son is eight years old and is in second grade, way too young, you think, to be questioning whether or not Santa is real, but there is no doubt that he is suspicious. You think that it is a shame that such a young boy is starting to be robbed of the magic that for you lasted through fifth grade. For the most part, you sort of ignore your son's questions on the topic of whether or not *you* are really Santa. You do not want to deceive him straight on and you do not want to raise his suspicions further by arguing too hard.

A week before Christmas, you are at a neighborhood holiday party—which, by the way, you were made aware of one half hour before leaving your house—and they have hired Santa to entertain this adult-only crowd. Of the many, he is one of the best Santas that you have seen at a party in the neighborhood. At this party, standing next to the fireplace mantel, you meet a woman. She is admiring all of the prominently displayed holiday cards featuring family upon family photographed at one exotic location after another. One says, "Happy Holidays from the Falalalalalalalangas."

After introducing yourself to her as Mark Falalalalalalalanga, she tells you that her young kids were once skeptical that Santa was real. "How did you address that issue?" you ask, looking for some clues. She tells you a story that intrigues you. Last year, she tells you, she hired the very Santa that is at this party to come into their home and distribute gifts. She said that after that her kids were totally convinced that Santa was real. Your wife, who gets even more excited about this holiday than you do, even though she never celebrated it as a child, gets an idea. That night, she hires Santa to come over to your house a week later, at 11 P.M. on Christmas Eve. It is her idea to set up the video camera with the kids earlier on Christmas Eve to see if they can capture Santa on film. You tell the kids that you are not sure if Santa will show up on video or not. You say that Santa, because of his magical qualities, may be invisible on the video. You do all of this in such a way that your kids think that all of this is their idea.

Your son thinks that he's got you now, because he has this brilliant idea, and if you are Santa, as he suspects you are, then you will be the one captured on that video film tomorrow morning, not Santa.

It is 9:30 P.M., Christmas Eve. The video is set up on a tripod and it is pointing at the tree. The kids go upstairs and get ready for bed. After reading together, you say a prayer (a Catholic one) and the kids go to sleep. At 11 P.M., Santa arrives, just as your wife had previously arranged. He is the best Santa that you have ever seen and he has shown up with a big sack. You brief him about your two children and you tell him what is in the packages that he will deliver. He earns the $80 he requests and you tip him $20.

The next morning, your kids wake you up and, like every Christmas morning, you all go barreling down the stairs to the living room together. Your kids open all of their presents, and as they are winding down your son remembers the video camera. He turns to the family and says, "Hey, let's see the video. Let's see if Santa came last night, let's see if he is real." You tell him that is a good idea. You rewind the video and press two or three buttons on the thing before you get it into play mode. You hope that you did not erase anything that may have been recorded the prior night.

For the next half hour on that video, you and your family witness something spectacular: the process of Santa delivering the wrapped gifts that your kids just opened. The grate of the fireplace rumbles. Santa is not yet in the view of the screen. But you can hear him. He talks to Rudolph, Prancer, and Dancer. He eats the cookies that your kids have left out for him and drinks his hot cocoa, plain as day. You hear the boxes rumble. In his thirty-minute performance, he talks specifically about both of your kids by name and he tells your kids to respect each other and to always try their best, while looking directly at the camera. He talks as he moves between the fireplace and the tree and places all of the gifts that your kids just opened. Your kids cannot believe what they have seen and your eight-year-old becomes his school's biggest Santa advocate. You have bought another year.

Get a New Computer

You have two computers in your house. One is your wife's 1984 Macintosh SE, so it doesn't really count. It is more like a souped-up Selectric typewriter, and even your children regard it as useless because it has no application for anything they are interested in—no Internet, no CD, no games. They cannot imagine what their mother uses it for.

You have another computer, which is now four years old, an eternity in computer years, which, in your mind, are like triple dog years, making your computer eighty-four years old. Your kids have a library of fifty, sixty—you don't know—seventy computer games, all on disks. You notice now that every time they insert one of these games it runs slowly, the sound stutters, the colors are weird, or the game doesn't open. The computer frequently sends you messages that the hard drive is full. "Not Enough Disk Space for This Application," it says. Not knowing much about computers, except the commonsense logic that you develop after years as a lightweight user, you think that if you delete things on your hard drive then everything will be OK. By OK, you mean that you will not be interrupted from whatever it is that you are doing anytime one of your kids turns on the computer to do something and gets frustrated because the computer is not doing what they want.

Typically in this situation you stop whatever you are doing, no matter what it is, and you start to deal with the source of your kids' frustration, the eighty-four-year-old computer. They call you and not your wife because you have billed yourself to your kids as a "dad who can fix anything." They know that your wife, who has not ventured beyond her 1984 Macintosh SE, will be useless in restoring their computer well-being. "My dad can fix anything," your daughter tells her friends, and that makes you feel good. Now it is time to deliver on that promise.

Your diagnostic inquiry starts with the easiest, most obvious thing: you take the CD out of the C or D drive—you are not really sure which one it is or what that really means—and you clean it with Windex. You insert the disk. Fifty percent of the time this cures the problem. This is the kind of repair that you like the most. On top of the fact that the computer now works, your kids have developed a newfound respect for you.

If that does not work, you begin dabbling in the unknown. The window that says "Not Enough Disk Space for This Application" concerns you. There is a ton of stuff loaded onto the computer, most of which was there when you turned the computer on when it came out of the box. You have been using this computer for eighty-four computer years and have not used most of these applications. You have no idea what most of them are and you are really not sure what impact deleting them will have on what you and your kids want to do on this computer. Nevertheless, you begin deleting files, once you accidentally figure out how to do so by finding a right-click mouse function. You wonder why this problem has never surfaced before, and tomorrow, when you are at work, you ask the Information Technology guy, Dan the computer man, and he tells you that the games now use more disk space and that your eighty-four-year-old computer no longer has the capacity to handle them. You sort of believe what this expert tells you, but not really. You think that somehow he will get a commission on a new computer that you buy and that that is his motivation for telling you that your eighty-four-year-old computer is not man enough to handle these new games.

After you have deleted just about everything from your computer and the new games that your kids want to run on the computer still do not work, you finally accept your fate.

That Christmas, Santa brings your family a new computer, which you all witness on videotape that Christmas morning after all the gifts are opened. It is a computer that you hope will free you up from being the family's Director of Information Technology. Your sole motivation in Santa bringing this new computer into your home is to give you a year or so of hassle-free computing. Santa brings the computer that Dan the computer man recommended. He ordered it for Santa and Santa ended up paying $400 more than Dan the computer man told him he would be paying. Asked several times if the kids' eighty or ninety existing computer games will play on the new computer, each time Dan responds, "Better than ever."

On Christmas morning, your kids open up the new computer. They are tingling with excitement at the thought of getting at those hundred or so games they have on CDs, which they haven't been able to play, in a hassle-free manner, for a year, give or take.

After all the excitement simmers down, it is time for you to set up the new computer. You have been told by Dan the computer man that all you need to do is plug it in and you are ready to go, a much simpler process than the last computer you bought. So that is what you do. You turn on the computer and the graphics are clear. Dan the computer man has told you that there will be absolutely no problems, that your new computer will have enough capacity to play any game. There will be a huge difference, he assures you.

Your kid inserts a CD of his choice. Nothing comes on. You calmly ask him to select another. No go. He tries a third, fourth, and fifth. All no-plays. You cannot believe what you are experiencing and you are tempted to call Dan the computer man on this Christmas morning to see what he got you into here. But you restrain yourself, mostly because you do not know how to get Dan's phone number.

You then tell your kids that even though their games do not work, they can go online and check out some games on the Internet. You try to get online but realize that Dan did not connect your Internet service, like he said he would. For that Christmas Friday and the following weekend, your kids have one brand-new computer that they can look at but not use, because it does not play any of their games, nor can they get online. It is about as useless to them as your wife's 1984 Macintosh SE. They have access to a second computer that does not have the capacity to play the games that they now want to play, and they have access to a third, a 1984 Macintosh SE, which they would like to dismantle to see what is inside to understand how computers were made in the olden days. While you are tempted to allow them to do that in order to make up for Santa screwing up so badly on this long Christmas weekend, you resist.

On Monday, you haul the brand-new computer that Santa brought into work. Dan the computer man is not in on that day. You leave the computer there overnight, and again disappoint the kids when you come home empty-handed. "Why was Dan the computer man allowed to take off today when you had to go to work?" your eldest asks.

The next day, Dan is back. He tells you that he had a wonderful Christmas. You do not want to hurt his feelings, so you say that you did, too. You tell him about some of the complications that you have experienced, the first being that you cannot get a game to work on the new computer that he specified for you.

Dan says, "No problem, let me take a look at it." He does, and he says, "Oh, this is Windows XP. That's the problem." "What does that mean?" you say. "The games that you have are all probably Windows 98 and 2000 compatible. They are not compatible with Windows XP," Dan says, clarifying the problem for you, but about a month too late.

"Dan," you ask, "does that mean what I think it means?" Dan tells you that none of the hundred and twenty or so games that you have will ever operate on this new computer. "XP is a more sophisticated operating system," he tells you, "and it is better than what you had on your old computer." You disagree.

That night, you drag the computer that you wish Santa had not brought your family back home. You describe what Dan has told you to the kids in a way that they can understand. "Let's go to Target, kids. We are going to get some new computer games," you say.

Go to Your Friends' House for Christmas Dinner

Your extended family lives in the suburbs of San Francisco and New York, respectively, and none are coming to visit you for Christmas this year, like they occasionally do. So Christmas dinner is a dilemma, until you are invited by your friends, or until your wife takes it upon herself to ask for an invitation, a point about which you will never gain full clarity. The friends, whose house you will visit for Christmas dinner, have never had anyone outside of their family join them for this special holiday event.

Like clockwork, an hour before you are supposed to arrive at your friends', the Sclafannis', your wife reveals to you the expected time of your arrival. You show up, and Joe Sclafanni's mother and brother are there along with his wife and kids. It's his entire immediate family . . . and you and your family. You met Joe on the sidelines of your kids' soccer games and since then he has become your close friend and business partner, with whom you buy, manage, and sell real estate.

You hang out first in the large kitchen. Eventually, you proceed to the large round dining-room table, which is set with all the right glasses, all the right plates, and all the right silverware in all the right places. It looks festive. There are water glasses, white-wine glasses, red-wine glasses (which are used most at this dinner table, where everyone seated has a vowel on the end of their last name), salad plates, bread plates, soup bowls, salad forks, dinner forks, soup spoons, and dessert spoons. This is a lot of stuff to keep track of, and, as in many meals of this nature, when there are many glasses and plates, for some it is confusing as to what is what and whose is whose.

The food is brought out in courses, and your hostess is a professional chef. You have scored big on this Christmas dinner. You are with good friends, you are hanging with their extended family (people's mothers always like you), and you are eating a world-class meal, created by a professional chef, that has been prepared on one of those $10,000 cast-iron industrial stoves, at a place setting that would be suitable for a $1,000-a-plate fund-raiser dinner. What could be better?

You are laughing and having a good time and are about halfway through the main course, moving through this gourmet dinner faster than anyone else sitting at the table, when all of a sudden your friend's wife turns to your wife and asks, loud enough to attract the attention of everyone sitting at the table, "Diane, what are you doing?" emphasizing each word in a discrete, staccato fashion. The question is asked in such a manner, with such surprise, so as to direct the attention of the entire table of guests to your wife. You wonder, has your wife taken her left breast out of her shirt? The laughing stops and everyone turns their attention to your wife. Your wife, who takes another gulp of water from her glass, which is three-quarters empty, before responding, says, "What are you talking about, Donna?"

Now, at the point that this question is posed to your wife, she is simply drinking water, her preferred beverage, out of what she believes to be her glass. In her mind, this mundane activity does not warrant such a question, asked with such emphasis. As organized a person as your wife is, she is a woman who often gets confused with these complex place settings as to which side her bread plate is on and which of the six or so glasses sitting to her right and left have been allocated to her. Her confusion with these matters, coupled with the confidence she exudes, is enough to set an entire table of diners out of whack, with everyone questioning whose glasses and bread plates belong to whom. Your wife, the center of attention of the entire table, is drinking her water out of the most enormous glass that any of you have ever seen in your lives.

Your wife, who you would say is more than comfortable having attention directed her way and who is very funny when it is, looks genuinely startled and says, "Donna, what is wrong?" She self-inspects, holding her glass away from her, in the air, so that she can see more of herself, expecting to see her left breast exposed, as she scoots away from the table a bit to see what Donna may be seeing. She cannot detect anything unusual or anything out of place. She is puzzled.

"Diane," Donna says, "you are drinking from the water pitcher." Your wife, who is seated next to you, looks at her "glass" and says again, "Donna, what are you talking about?" "That's the water pitcher," Donna repeats. You and everyone else at the table take stock of this situation, and, sure enough, Donna is right. Your wife, perhaps thinking that she was the honored guest, assumed that she was served water in the extra-big glass, a carafe-sized "glass" that was way bigger than any other glass on the table. The glass that, your wife admits to everyone, was a little awkward to drink from because that funny protrusion, the lip of the pitcher, kept interfering with the smooth transfer of water from this serving container into her mouth.

Your wife, at this juncture, has two ways in which she could react, but only one comes to her mind. Option one is that she get embarrassed in front of this warm extended family that she is meeting on this occasion for this special Christmas dinner that for the first time opened up this special holiday to nonfamily members. This, of course, is not your confident wife's style. In the nineteen years that you have known your wife, you have never seen her embarrassed in any situation; you do not anticipate this reaction from her today, and you are not let down.

Option two is that she make a joke of it, which she does well. She tells you all that early on, when she noticed that the largest and most formidable glass at the table was placed before her, she assumed that she was being welcomed into this family as an *extra*-special guest. She told everyone that she thought it was an Italian tradition, an "Italian custom at Christmas," she said, a way to welcome nonfamily guests. She told everyone that she was wondering what all of these other glasses were for, given the fact that the one that was placed directly in front of her was so large and had the capacity to hold as much beverage as all the others sitting in front of her combined. She told you that she questioned why anyone would drink from those small glasses when there was such a large glass.

Everyone laughed and laughed uncontrollably and since then you all have been invited back for Christmas dinner with the Sclafannis each year. Your wife can always find her place setting at this dinner table. It is the one with the really, really large glass of water sitting in front of it.

Go to a New Year's Party

It is New Year's, and there are many parties that you are invited to. In some respects, it is a difficult night, because when you RSVP you want to do so in a timely way but you also want to hedge your bets and maintain your flexibility in the event that a better invitation comes along.

You, of course, are not consulted in this process, as your wife, for this first night of the year, is making the plans without your input, just as she has done all of last year and will do all this year and the next. Why should this first night, you ask, be different than any other night? You know one resolution that your wife is *not* making this New Year.

Forty-five minutes before you have to leave the house, your wife informs you that you will be going over to the Girards' that night. You think that this sounds pretty good. You enjoy parties at the Girards'. They are informal and they attract your core group and then some others. You are grateful on this night that your wife has notified you an additional fifteen minutes earlier than she usually does for events of this nature.

You go to the Girards' and find that a good crowd is there. The energy is good, there are a lot of kids running around, and there are many people from your core group. You can kick back and enjoy it all. Gary always has some good red wine, and on this first night of the New Year you enjoy that. You roam from room to room. You get tired of listening to one guy, who you just met, talk about his job, so you move on with the excuse that you need a refill. You circulate and you think about how you like this style of party more than most others. You are a free agent, you can meander in and out of conversations as you please.

It is 10:15 and your wife comes over to see how you are doing. You tell her that you think that this is a terrific party and that you are so happy that she selected this party to come to. You tell her that this will be a fun place to be at midnight and that the kids, with many of their friends, are having a blast. To this your wife responds, "Honey, we have to go over to the Jensens' now. We were supposed to be there fifteen minutes ago." You think that she has had as much wine to drink as you have and that she is goofing you with this news, but then you remember that she does not drink wine and her "Come on, let's get over there now" expression tells you that you are on your way. "The kids can stay," she tells you. The Jensens' is not a kid party, and that is the first clue that the Jensens' party will be different from the Girards'.

On the drive over to the Jensens', you ask your wife what this party is all about and you ask why she double-booked on New Year's. Before she gets a chance to answer the question you asked, you are at the front door and Alyssa Jensen opens it for you. You walk in and everyone you see is dressed in ties, sport coats, some suits even, and evening dresses. Everyone is seated at formal place settings. The average age in the living/dining room, where people are seated formally with extensive place settings before them, is at least fifteen years older than the average age of you and your wife, who is five years your junior.

Alyssa directs you through the dining room, past an entire dining table full of people whom you do not recognize, into the living room, where there are three round tables of about ten people each, whom you do not recognize. She directs you to the center table and points to a place setting with your name on it and then escorts your wife to the opposite side of the table. You are seated between two people you have never seen before, and you are committed. You are no longer free to roam and you are no longer a free agent. Your host, who is really funny, who you would like to be seated with, is sitting at one of the other tables. He is too far away to talk to, and his funny commentary will be out of your audible range. There is wine on each table that you assume came from Russell's wine cellar, and for that you are happy. You know that the wine Russell serves from his cellar is stronger than most others and you hope that trend continues tonight. You fill up your glass to the brim.

You are next to a man who lives two suburbs away and owns a large contracting business. Having confirmed his hunch that you work for a large real-estate company, he goes on to tell the entire table that fifteen years ago he built out an office for a company that no longer exists in one of the buildings that you manage. He announces to your entire table how unaccommodating your building was to his firm during that project, before you were there, and how terrible it was to do work there. He makes some analogy to the mob after you have stopped listening.

You detest these comments, in part because you have committed the past ten years of being a corporate executive to making this building one of the most accommodating places of its kind anywhere. His story is stale and is further from the truth now as it was then, but there is no way to convince this man of that fact. He is set in his thinking, is insistent that everyone at your table understand his point of view, and at a New Year's Eve party you do not want to ring in the New Year by defending the building that you manage. You are through listening to this man, but you know now that he will not do work in this office building ever again.

You turn to your left and start talking with the woman who is seated next to you, who lives in another suburb. She does nothing but complain about her house, how this room is not quite right and how they can never get the water to the right temperature. You tire of listening to this rich person talk of her petty, fabricated hardships. You look to your wife, who realizes, like you do, that you are into the first of many courses of this dinner. There is no way out.

A sparkle comes to your wife's eye. Two minutes later, she informs the table that she absolutely must go back to the Girards' and put your five-year-old daughter, who is under the weather, to bed. She leaves. You are flying solo between Mr. Contractor and Mrs. Million-Dollar-House-Is-Not-Quite-Right. Twenty minutes later, the Jensens' phone rings. Alyssa, the hostess, taps you on the shoulder and informs you that you must go home immediately, that your under-the-weather daughter is overly tired and is demanding that she see Daddy.

You smile inside and look rushed as you leave, like you are on some big, important mission. You get into the suburban cab that you called from the Jensens' and get driven to the Girards' and you are once again a free man, a man of flow, roaming from room to room. That first night, your entire family rings in the New Year together.

See Holiday Lights in Your Neighborhood

It is early February. It gets dark at 4:45 P.M. and it is cold. Because it is cold, you run into few of your neighbors except for David Golob, who, over the course of the winter, will tell you on at least sixteen occasions that he loves you. In winter, people move purposefully from their detached garages to their houses. Very few people are out for walks or bike rides. Your suburb is dormant.

You think back fondly on how warm and cheerful the neighborhood looked just two short months ago. Most of the houses were decorated with colorful holiday lights. Conifer trees on front lawns were wrapped in lights capped with stars, and houses were decorated like wedding cakes, with those new icicle lights that everyone in your suburb seems to prefer now over the older-style, single-strand lights.

In late December, you spend a lot of time driving around the neighborhood with your family marveling at the decorated houses. Most people in your suburb are fairly moderate in their approach to holiday home decorating. You attribute that to the fact that most people have better things to do with their time than climb ladders in the dead of winter to string lights that usually don't work until you jiggle them just right. To your surprise, professional light decorators, for some reason, have not yet emerged in your suburb. You suspect they will someday.

You reminisce with your family about how beautiful and warm all those house decorations make your suburb feel, even though they are not nearly as elaborate as they are in a city neighborhood where you take your family each holiday season. In that neighborhood, a place that you refer to as the suburb-in-the-city, a culture has developed that seems to encourage people to go all out with their decorations in a kind of competition. It is February 2 and now all those holiday lights are down. Even the Philips', whom you remember calling last year on the evening of February 11, when you drove by their house after picking up your daughter from a playdate at the Fords' to inform them that Christmas was over.

You yearn for that season again, the season when all these houses, which now look so bleak, could come to life again with their sparkly, colorful lights. But you come to the sad realization that you have another eleven months before this special time of year rolls around again.

Wait a minute, not so fast: the night when you see the neighborhood lit up with optimism and life may not be as far away as you think. You remember the Franz house. Of all the neighbors in your suburb, the Franzes take their holiday decorating most seriously. The unconfirmed rumor is that Mr. Franz owns his own electrical-contracting business. That is one plausible reason why this house radiates with lights on every square inch of its surface. Another is that the Franzes moved to your suburb from the suburb-in-the-city and brought their house-decorating culture along with them. This is a house that is always decorated; it is a house that is just a canvas for lights. For the Franzes, every day presents an occasion to have their house decorated so as to delight the neighbors, though you are not so sure that everyone is so delighted, especially their across-the-street neighbors.

On this particular day, you count the days after the last holiday and before the next one. You recall that, no matter what the evening, the Franzes' home is always lit up. One holiday transitions into another. For any given holiday there are phases of decorations, with the first phase often being more excessive than anything that anyone else in the neighborhood will do. There are usually at least three phases until the final effect of lights and decorations is achieved.

Before you know it, Christmas turns into a winter-wonderland theme, where Santa, his reindeer, the illuminated snowman, the candy canes, the workshop, the elves, the gifts, and the Noel sign affixed to the roof give way to fully wrapped deciduous trees and a partial house wrap with the words "Happy Winter" emblazoned on the roof, in place of "Noel." Before you know it, it is mid-January, and not too early to begin thinking about Valentine's Day. The white lights give way to red ones, which cover the house and the trees, and the hedges are wrapped with hearts.

A week after Valentine's Day, the red lights start turning green. At first you are puzzled, thinking that there is a reversion back to Christmas, before you remember St. Patrick's Day. Over the next week, the red is gone and everything is lit up green. Green shamrocks and illuminated leprechauns are everywhere. You wonder if Franz is an Irish name, which would help explain all this enthusiasm for the good St. Patrick.

After the seventeenth, big bunnies start populating the lawn and roof. Baskets of Easter eggs, as tall as the first two stories of the house, are placed on the front lawn. The Easter theme then transitions to a May spring theme. Lit-up flowers and vertical rows of white colored lights, which you imagine represent a May shower, decorate the house. But then you remember that the showers are in April—April showers; May flowers, stupid—and you become confused at those vertical strands of white lights, not knowing what they represent.

It's June, and Flag Day is coming up. Red, white, and blue dominate and you assume the theme will carry the house through to the Fourth of July, but you are wrong. An entirely different red-white-and-blue theme emerges, with lights fanning out as they reach the roofline, representing fireworks. You excitedly await the August transition, but the Franzes have not been successful yet in figuring out how to choreograph their August light theme. Either that or they are on vacation.

You would think that the savings on the Commonwealth Edison electric bill would extend through mid-September, but you are proven wrong when during the third week of September the first phase of orange lights emerges. Over the next week and a half, pumpkins, witches, goblins, and ghosts crop up in three phases.

November brings on the turkeys, Pilgrims, and cornucopia filled with inflated corn on the cob as long as the front walk.

Then the big one, Phase I of Christmas, commences on December 1.

On this second day of February, when you want to experience the visual warmth of house lights, you pile your family in the car and drive by the Franzes'. You see the hearts and red lights and you think to yourself how glad you are that you did not buy the Metcalfs' house, which is directly across the street.

Go Black-Light Bowling

There is a windowless bowling alley in your suburb. The owners, a couple who each time you have seen them are wearing
tie-dyed Grateful Dead T-shirts, fixed it up a bit and put black
lights everywhere. There are many kids' birthday parties in this
bowling alley, especially for kids who were born in the winter.

Once a year or so, you get together with a group of your
friends to bowl and drink beer. These nights are fun, but it always surprises you that these evenings are initiated and planned
by the women in the group, because black lights make anything
that is white or brightly colored look like it is glowing. That is
the whole idea of black-light bowling; the effect looks cool and
it is an effect that most people do not use in their homes, not
even the Franzes, who seem to display every kind of light
imaginable. The interesting thing about black lights, you learn
after attending your first adults' party at the black-light bowling
alley, is that the black lights pick up on hair that is dyed blond,
but *not* naturally blond hair. You realize for the first time that
pretty much every woman in your social circle dyes her hair
blond, and you know this because just about every woman's
hair glows in this black-light bowling alley. You do not see any

guy that you know with glowing hair, not yet, anyway, but just about every woman has it.

A group of women with glowing hair has formed in a tight conversational circle by Lane 4, and you suspect that they may be discussing how embarrassed they feel because of their glowing hair. Having a sudden interest in bowling on Lane 3, you curiously walk by this recently formed glowing ring of women to see exactly how embarrassed they really are about their hair, only to overhear them making plans for next year's black-light bowling night.

Go Ice Skating with Your Friends

You grew up playing hockey, and every boy you knew who skated when you were growing up skated on hockey skates, except three boys named Charlie, Jim, and Ted, who skated on figure skates, and who as adults preferred to be called Charles, James, and Theodore.

As an ex-hockey player, you have no other choice than to bring your boy up skating with hockey skates. This rule is part of an unspoken code that all hockey players share. Except one, your friend Rick.

One Saturday, you and your daughter meet Rick, his wife, and their kids at an outdoor rink. Your son is home sick and is bummed out that he is not there with you and you are bummed out that there was no reason to bring him to his swim lesson with Annika today. Like you, Rick played hockey growing up. Like you, hockey was Rick's No. 1 sport, and, unlike you, Rick now plays hockey in a men's league and last year played a game with the New York Rangers, for which you assume he paid a massive sum of money. You suspect that he is a better hockey player than you, but this is something that you will never, ever admit to him.

All this hockey in your friend Rick's blood had a strong influence on Rick naming his only son Cooper, after the world's largest manufacturer of hockey equipment. Cooper is the brand of hockey stick, shin pads, hockey pants, shoulder pads, elbow pads, helmet, gloves, and jerseys that you and every other hockey player wore when you were growing up. It is a market-dominating brand.

Rick is the last person you think would have his kid, Cooper, named after the world's leading hockey-equipment maker, wearing figure skates. No worries here. Today, however, you learn that about that assumption you could not be more wrong.

On this beautiful five-degree day, you show up to skate. You go into the warming house, where a fire is burning in the fireplace, and you greet your friends. You say hello to your daughter's good friend Emma and hug Rick's wife and shake Rick's hand. Cooper, who you suspected would be decked out in a $150 set of CCM Tacks, is not.

You go to give Cooper a fake high five, where you pull your hand away at the last minute, like you always do, because it makes him laugh, and you notice something that you are not prepared for. What you observe catches you so off guard that you forget to pull your hand away to fake Cooper out, because this boy, this hockey-player-to-be, this hockey legacy, is wearing figure skates. Not only are they figure skates; *they are white figure skates.*

"Rick," you say, "what's up with the skates? They are really nice. No, really, I mean it," you say. Rick's wife, Beth, who has known you long enough to understand your ability to poke fun, steps in to defend your friend Rick. "Cooper's ice-skating teacher said that Cooper should start skating on figure skates," she says. "Did his skating instructor specifically recommend *white* figure skates?" you ask. You do not get an answer. Rick's wife tells you to stop discussing Cooper's skates in front of him, because he may get self-conscious about them. "Wouldn't Cooper getting self-conscious about wearing white figure skates be a good thing?" you ask. Again, you receive no reply. You look to Rick and comment that it may be time to reconsider his wife's selection of a skating instructor for his son Cooper.

The next day, you run into Rick's wife on the train coming home from work. You are seated three seats behind the only person in your car who is sitting alone, and "she" has long, flowing blond hair, is wearing high-heeled shoes, has two-inch-diameter hoop earrings, is wearing black stretch bell-bottom pants and high heels, and has long manicured fingernails that are painted black.

Beth tells you that when Cooper came home from skating yesterday he tried on his sister's dress. "So what did you expect?" you say. From the train station, you walk home with Beth and you tell her to come into your house for a minute, that you have something for her. Beth comes in, and hangs out in the kitchen with your wife while you run to the garage. You enter your garage and David Golob's garage door starts to open. In the garage, you find your son's first pair of skates, a pair of *black* hockey skates, and give them to Rick's wife and say, "Beth, please give Cooper these skates, *now*."

Go for a Walk with Your Wife

It is 3:45 P.M. on Sunday and your son is at basketball practice. It ends at 5:15 and his friend's dad, your friend Mitch Larson, is driving him home. Your daughter is at her friend Emma's for a playdate. Your wife has made arrangements for her to stay there until 5 P.M. or so. You are a free man and wife for an hour and fifteen.

This is an unusual circumstance to experience in the middle of the day. You come into the house and your wife says to you, "We have an hour and fifteen minutes alone—would you like to go for a walk?" You think of some other things that you would like to do with your wife, but this sounds pretty good. It is winter, it is below-zero cold, there are massive icebergs down at the beach, and you love going to the beach more than you like most things, all year round. Your wife knows this, like she knows you love purple grape juice. What better place, you think, to take a walk than on the beach.

You say, "Honey, that sounds terrific. That is a great idea." You get your long johns on and she hers. You get your coats on and you say, "Let's drive to the beach and then walk along the beach." It takes you three minutes to drive to the beach, including the time it takes to walk from your house into the garage, get into the car, open the garage door, pull out of the garage, and close the garage door. (That is one reason you overpaid so much for your house.)

Who can argue about a walk along the beach, especially someone who has already established that she wants to go for a walk. You say, "Let's go," not wanting to waste a precious moment. As you walk out the back door of your house, your wife says to you, "I wanted to walk in the neighborhood. Why don't we walk *to* the beach," emphasizing the *to*. You are accustomed to being challenged frequently about many ideas you introduce into your household, but your idea to drive to and then walk along the beach is one about which you were not anticipating any resistance. In your mind, it is just not a topic that should be controversial at all.

You soon realize that you are wrong about this. You walk to the car while your wife says two more times, "I just felt like walking from here." "Honey," you say, "let's just go to the beach. We see our neighborhood every time we leave and return from our home. The beach is amazing now. There are so many huge ice floes. It's such a great opportunity to check it out."

She says "OK" and reluctantly gets in the car. As you are pulling out of your garage, David Golob's garage door begins to open. You drive through the alley and onto the curved street.

By this time, the topic of *where* to take your walk has become the single most important issue of your wife's existence. She says to you again, in a more assertive way, "I just wanted to start walking from home!"

You fail to see any logic in your wife's assertiveness on this topic, but you know better than to try to understand her logic. It is the same logic, you believe, that she deployed for seven years in not buying you your favorite beverage. At least she is consistent, you think to yourself, for whatever that is worth.

You wish more than anything that in a situation like this your wife could just flow with it. You wish that in matters as meaningless as taking a walk she could for once just accept your idea. You wish that, to your wife, just spending time with you *anywhere* would be a good enough way to spend an hour and fifteen minutes. But on this day, like most, your wishes do not come true. You know your wife well enough to know that the only thing to do now is turn around, park the car in the garage, and start your walk from the house. This is what you do. "Whatever will make you happy, honey," you say unenthusiastically.

As in most situations like this, the only thing to do is to get over it and put it out of your mind quickly. You start walking from your house and walk to the beach, along the beach, and back home. It is a terrific walk, and what you enjoy most is spending the time with your wife.

Drive

You live in a suburb with brick streets. It is an old neighborhood. Most of the houses have only two garage spaces. Because
there is a lot of disposable income in this suburb, when kids
turn fifteen and sixteen they get cars, which for the most part
are indistinguishable from their parents' cars. Because there are
generally only two garage spaces per house, these third and
fourth cars in the household end up parked on the street. You
do not like this parked-on-the-street look, and neither do
others, but there is not much to be done about it, until one day
you have an idea.

A few years ago, when you began observing cars parked on
the street in front of your house, you asked your son and his
friends if they would like to play baseball on the front lawn.
"You have plenty of space to play," you said to them. "Don't
worry about the cars, you won't hit them." They did play with
the brand-new hardball that you had given them to use, but
occasionally the cars did get in the way of the balls the kids hit.
Since the advent of those baseball games, there have never
again been cars parked on the street on *your* block. You suspect
that they have relocated to other streets. Anytime the cars start

parking there again, your kid and his friends get a sudden urge to play baseball on the front lawn.

Because the streets were built long ago, they are not as wide as you would find in other, newer suburbs that have been built over cornfields. While there are many cars parked on one side of many of your suburban streets, because parking is restricted on the other side, there is still always room for your car and an opposing car to drive by. The streets are dimensioned adequately to fit three cars across. You know this, but most of the drivers in oncoming cars do not. They think that the streets are too narrow, so either they will pull to the side and stop to let you go by, or will expect you to do that for them. You are also usually in a rush to get somewhere, so, to you, every minute counts. Like eating, showering, and shopping, driving is something that you like to do fast. You realize that if you stopped and pulled to the side to let each opposing car pass you it would take twice as long to get most places in your neighborhood. Long ago you made the decision to keep on driving when you confront this frequently occurring situation, because you know that, while tight, there is enough room for everyone.

This decision, like many you make, has positive and negative consequences. On the positive side, you get places quickly and your driving is steady. On the downside, you are the recipient of a lot of nasty looks from people who generally recognize you or your car as you barely squeeze by each other. You have learned to avoid eye contact when you fail to stop for oncoming traffic on these brick suburban streets. You can tell that the person, usually a mom, in the opposing car, typically an oversized Suburban or Navistar, usually thinks that because they are proceeding along a section of street with cars parked on one side that you, the oncoming car, should pull over to the curb or between two parked cars and stop to let them pass by. You don't, and you know that it does not matter, because the street is wide enough to accommodate all of you, even the Suburban, and that everyone always makes it by OK, even though it is a tight fit.

You have accepted these nasty looks as a consequence of a decision you have made, but you always hope that they are from people who do not know you or recognize you. You are never quite sure, though, because it has been a long time since you have made eye contact with anyone driving in a vehicle that is coming toward you on your suburban streets.

Convert to Premium Gasoline

Your German luxury car has a stick shift. You really enjoy your time in this car, because you think that there is no car that is better suited to you than this one, which is responsive to your aggressive driving style.

Fifteen years ago, the day after you got your first real job offer, you bought your first nice car from the car dealer whom you liked so much you wanted to invite him to your wedding. It was a Swedish luxury car with a stick shift, and you liked it even though it needed to be fixed often. Luckily, you found a mechanic that you really trusted.

Your mechanic was this good guy named Kevin but who referred to himself as Sven. Sven, who you called Kevin, was the smartest mechanic you ever met. He worked only on the brand of Swedish cars that have a reputation for needing a lot of work. For Sven, choosing this brand of car to center a business on was no random, haphazard event. He knew that these cars need a lot of TLC, and that their owners were loyal to the brand and liked them to run at peak performance. He figured that he could make more money repairing this particular brand of car than any other car, and, if he made half as much from his other customers as he did from you, you know he was right and that he was living big.

One day, you ask Sven what type of gasoline you should use in your car. You believe him to be *the most qualified* person to answer this question. He does not hesitate with his response, and there is no lack of confidence in his voice. Sven tells you that your car will run the same on any octane level commonly available at any gas station. You have been paying the twenty cents per gallon upcharge for the expensive stuff for a year or so, since you purchased your first new car, so Sven's response means money in your pocket from now on. This is a good news day. You immediately stop buying the expensive stuff and switch to the lowest grade of regular.

You drive that car for 102,000 miles before you sell it and trade up to a German luxury car with a stick shift. During the new-car orientation when you pick up your German luxury car from the dealer—whom you do not like as much as the dealer from whom you purchased your Swedish luxury car—your car dealer tells you to use only premium gasoline. You nod your head yes, knowing that you will not; someone more insightful than him has told you to save your money. You assume that car dealers have some kind of conspiracy going with gas stations and get some kind of "commission" from them based on the difference between the price of premium gasoline and the price of the cheapest stuff, which Sven told you to buy.

You pull off the lot and the first thing you do is fill up that new German luxury car with regular gasoline. It runs fine, you think, much better than your 102,000-mile Swedish luxury car. After all, it is a German luxury car with 2.8 miles on it. You continue to buy regular gasoline for the five years that you own that car, and for your next new car you acquire, which happens to be of the same brand. You are now fifteen years into driving these fancy European cars and you have bought only the cheapest-grade gasoline that you can buy because of that one conversation with Sven, years ago.

Then, one day, you come home from a business trip that you have taken with your friend-boss to one of the properties your company owns in High Point, North Carolina. It is night, and Sean, one of the security guards in the building that you manage in Chicago, picks you up in the less than a year old Lincoln Continental that your company owns. You and your friend-boss sit in the back and you talk about the day and ask Sean how his day was. Sean usually does not speak much on these trips home from the airport. That is, until he drops your friend-boss off at his big house, which sits on two lots. It is funny, you notice, that once your friend-boss leaves the car Sean starts talking to you about all kinds of stuff. This happens every time Sean gives you and your friend-boss a ride home from the airport, which is at least once a week.

On this night, as you pull out of the long driveway of this ample home which sits on the only double lot in this highest-income-per-capita suburb—which, as you have once been corrected by one of its residents, is actually a village—Sean all of a sudden has something on his mind that he wants to share with you. He becomes talkative.

"Could you believe how shitty this car is driving?" he asks. You tell him that you have not really noticed. "Check this out," he responds, as he nails it on this quaint, short, highest-income-per-capita in the U.S. street, where you have never seen anyone drive faster than twenty-five mph. The car sputters and hesitates badly. You admit that you notice the problem then and it is not good. "What is wrong?" you ask. Sean responds, "We hired some new security guard who wanted to save our $11-billion, 75-million-square-foot real-estate company a few bucks by buying regular-grade gasoline instead of premium grade. That is why this car is fucked up. Could you believe what that idiot has done? Would you ever do that to *your* car?"

At that point, your interest in this conversation picks up, and you ask, "Will the car always be fucked up, or will it go back to performing better once you put in the expensive gasoline?" You ask this question not because you care about the car you are in at that moment, but you know that the answer to this question will impact you and the German luxury car that you drive. Sean says, "I don't know."

You are now at your house. That night after supper, you get in your car to go to the library with your son. You decide to swing by the gas station and fill your car up with the most expensive gasoline they have. That night, the ride from the gas station to the library is the smoothest, snappiest ride that you have had in any of your cars in the past fifteen years.

Go to a Restaurant with Your Family

It is Sunday evening, and this weekend, like most, was event-packed. There was a soccer game, ballet class, swimming lessons (with Annika), your son's football game, two playdates, a birthday party for your daughter to attend, and a Cub Scout activity. This afternoon, your wife asked if you felt like going out to dinner tonight.

Your wife makes gourmet meals just about every night of the week, and when she asks if you feel like going to a restaurant you tend to think that she is feeling tapped out and in need of a break. "Great idea," you respond. "That sounds like fun."

Your wife asks where you would like to go. Of course, she has already thought this through in her mind and knows exactly where she would like to go, but why miss out on an opportunity to arrive at a common solution together? She asks this question, hopeful that you will somehow stumble upon the same idea that she has, but, if you don't, she knows that she can effectively manipulate your thinking to align it with hers, making it seem like somehow the restaurant that you end up at was your idea when it fact you had nothing to do with the selection.

"Bruno's," you respond, naming one of your favorite family restaurants, a lively nearby place that has terrific pasta, which is your favorite food. You have been there only twice, both times when your wife has been out on "girls' night." Your wife looks at you as though you have just recommended going to the lunch counter at Target for dinner. "Bruno's," she says. "I am tired of Bruno's. You always want to go there. Where else?" she asks. "What about the Mexican Café?" you suggest. "No," she says. "I don't feel like Mexican." You now start to understand that you are really playing a game of twenty questions, and that, unless you stumble upon the one restaurant that your wife has already selected for you, you will have to continue suggesting restaurants until you stumble across it. Alternatively, it may be a game of process of elimination, whereby your wife's strategy is to eliminate any option that you introduce, leaving only one logical alternative, the place where she wants to go. You say to your wife, "You know, honey, I really don't care where we go. Where would *you* like to go?"

Having already addressed this issue in her own mind, your wife responds to your inquiry instantly. In a nanosecond she says, "Let's go to *Ho Sing*." She says this loud enough for the kids to hear so that they get excited about the prospect of eating with chopsticks and eating food that they like. She deploys this strategy because she knows that the last place that you would ever suggest would be a Chinese restaurant. Over the past nineteen years that you have known each other, you have never once introduced the idea of going to a Chinese restaurant, nor, over that same period of time, have you ever responded favorably to anyone's recommendation to go to a Chinese restaurant. There is nothing that you really find appealing about this type of food, and you have never really understood all the to-do around it. You think that it is gooey and greasy and you have never really stumbled upon a favorite dish.

The only aspect of Chinese food that you find at all redeeming is that you can order the food simply by calling out a number.

At this point, it is three to one and you and your wife know that if you reject this idea of going Chinese, as they say, you will be the most unpopular dad in your suburb. You look at your wife and she knows that she has you. "That sounds great," you reply untruthfully. "I really feel like Chinese tonight. What a terrific idea."

It is 5 P.M., an hour before your usual dinnertime, but for some reason your wife believes that the kids are famished. "Let's go immediately," she says. "Everyone get your shoes on. We are going now." The restaurant is a five-minute drive away, yet on the way out of the house your wife believes your kids to be so hungry—she always believes they are hungry—that she gives them a snack of licorice. "Honey," you say, "why would you give them a snack now? We'll be at the restaurant in five minutes. They could wait." "They are hungry," she says.

Just as your kids are finishing their snack, you arrive at the restaurant and park the SUV. En route, you drive by two cars, one after another, and you notice, out of the corner of your eye, that both drivers scowl at you. By not making eye contact with them, you do not give them the satisfaction of knowing that they think you are being an asshole.

You walk into the restaurant and are seated. Unlike in the restaurants that you prefer most, there will be no bread and olive oil served before dinner tonight. You sit down in a booth, but, according to your wife, you have selected the wrong seat. "You better sit on the inside," she says to you, "so Blake can get out and go to the bathroom if he needs to." You know that your wife knows that your son is fully capable of asking you to move in the event that he has to go to the bathroom and that you can quite capably get out of his way if such an event arises, but you do not bother to initiate this discussion with your wife.

You simply switch seats with your son, because that is the alternative that will put you on the path of least resistance. (He, too, knows that the alternative to relocating his seat is not worth the effort.) Your wife nervously looks around for the waiter, who arrives and asks if you would like something to drink. She responds, "I am famished and our kids are, too. We need food now." The waiter, understanding that the flow for this meal will be different than the flow for any other meals that he will serve that night, and most other nights, for that matter, responds as he should. "Would you like to order?" Well, you have just sat down, and with this cue you pick up your menu. It has items numbered from 1 to 128, and then some others that are not numbered. It is somewhat overwhelming to you, until you remember that to you most of this food tastes the same and most of it has that same gooey texture. You do not become that invested in the menu.

Your wife looks to you and asks if you are ready to order. Not really, you think, but you know better. That is your cue to give your wife more time to make her selections. You raise up your index finger to the waiter, indicating "One minute, please," hoping that you did not just flip him off in Chinese. You look more closely at the menu and still have difficulty distinguishing one dish from another and then order No. 14, because the combined age of your kids is fourteen. You ask for a Chinese beer to drink as well.

While you were going through this with the waiter, your wife has been conferring with your kids and seems to have narrowed down her choices. Surprisingly, each of your kids has a strong preference. You ask if they will order, and they do. First, your son says to the waiter, "Could I please have egg rolls and fried rice?" and your daughter asks for fried rice, please. They make you proud that they do this so politely.

Your wife is up, and, if tradition holds, there will be a rather lengthy and involved discussion with the waiter about the various options. She asks for the waiter's dinner recommendations and advice because, though she doesn't consider you to be an expert in office furniture, she sees the waiter as the source and authority of the highest-quality, most unbiased information, rather than how you see him, as a man trying to up the bill and increase his tip potential as best he can.

There is discussion about fish and cashew chicken, various types of spring rolls, and sauces with which you are unfamiliar. Finally, your wife asks the waiter what fish dish he would recommend. "Number thirty-eight," he says automatically. Your wife refers to her menu and it looks good to her. You glance at the menu that your waiter has not yet taken from you and notice that, of all 128 items on this menu, No. 38 wins in the most expensive category, by a good 30 percent. "Perfect," your wife says. "That looks really delicious."

The waiter takes the menus from all of you, and your wife adds, "The kids are starving. Could you please bring anything out that is ready for them as soon as possible?" In time, less than you anticipated, three people emerge from a double swinging door, which you assume is the dividing line between the kitchen and dining room. They have plates of food in hand, which you think may belong to your family. The food is yours, and 75 percent of your four-person family is very excited. There are special chopsticks, bound at the top with rubber bands and paper so that the kids can control them. They love the experience of eating with this infrequently used utensil. Your wife believes that she has ordered the best item on the menu, because it has been endorsed by your waiter. By its price, you agree. You, however, have struck out again. Your plate, containing menu item No. 14, is saturated with a brown, viscous, translucent, Valvoline-like substance that is covering what you guess to be vegetables, chicken, and sticky white rice.

To be part of the family experience, you eat a little, but

mostly you enjoy everyone else enjoying themselves. The question that you have always had about this food, wondering what people see in it, remains. You pick through your food but mostly leave it alone. Your Chinese beer, you come to accept, will be the highlight of this meal for you.

Your family finishes their food and everyone is ready to go. Your wife, eager to leave, flags down the waiter and asks for the check. You take it and begin reaching for your money. Your wife asks you to leave a tip, which is a good thing, because this is the first time in your life that you have ever eaten at a restaurant and paid, so you are not familiar with the custom of leaving a tip.

You return home, and just as you pull into the garage the Golobs' garage door opens. You rush your family into the house. As a family unit, you are 75 percent satisfied with that dinner. You enter the kitchen, get out a pot, put some water in it, bring it to a boil, and cook some spaghetti noodles. You cook them just right, pour some sauce on them, and sit down to eat a real meal.

Select a Video with Your Wife

Your kids are asleep and it is 8:30 P.M. It is a perfect evening to stay at home and rent a video or DVD. One day about nine months ago, you noticed when you went into Blockbuster that 90 percent of the selections were DVDs, not videos, which you had been accustomed to renting. The time before that when you went into this store, it seemed like their selection was better suited to your hardware capabilities, in that videos accounted for 90 percent of the selections. You get the hint. You are a man with flow and you go out and buy two DVD players for the TVs in your house where you do your movie watching.

That night, you and your wife think that it would be fun to rent one or the other. It doesn't matter now, because your family is current with its equipment. You are a home-movie switch-hitter. You look at the pile of dirty dishes on the kitchen table and say to your wife, "Honey, I don't want to trouble you with going to the video store on this cold evening. I will go out."

She goes to one of her pads of paper and jots down the title of a video that her friend Robin told her about that morning. As she hands you a small folded slip of paper with her movie selection, she says, "Why don't you get this; Robin recommended it, and she always recommends something that *you* enjoy." What your wife just told you is that this will be some sentimental love story in which someone is dying of cancer. Your wife will cry and be sad throughout the movie and you will be wishing that you were upstairs doing something more enjoyable with your time, like trying to figure out why your stock portfolio dropped by 30 percent over the past year. She hands you the folded scrap of paper, which you slip into your pocket while looking for your shoes, which your wife has relocated since you took them off a half hour ago.

"Great, honey," you say, trying to get out of there as soon as possible, before your wife changes her mind and wants to go, leaving you with the dishes. "Could you pick up a gallon of two percent milk?" your wife requests as you leave the house.

You are thinking that you would like to see *Day of the Jackal*, but you know that this is not a movie that Robin would recommend, therefore it will not be a movie that makes your wife's list of must-sees.

You arrive at Blockbuster. One thing that you enjoy is walking around the store and looking at every title and reading the description of every movie. After doing this, you like to select what you think is the best one. Usually, after spending forty-five minutes selecting the perfect movie, you get home and one of three things occurs. One is that the movie that you took too much time selecting is one that your wife does not want to see. Alternatively, you have selected a movie that, when you start viewing it, you both realize that you have seen before. The third possibility is that you have taken so long to select a movie that when you get home your wife has initiated another activity and she no longer wants to watch a movie, so you end up watching some chick flick like *Terms of Endearment*, which you have selected with your wife's interests in mind, on your own.

Tonight, you vow to yourself on the drive over—while squeezing between an oncoming SUV, whose driver's eyes you avoid, and a parked German luxury car—that you will get whatever is on that little piece of paper that your wife has handed to you and will be back home in five minutes, so that, unlike other movie evenings, this one will be a success, for your wife, anyway.

You park the car, enter the store, and pull the little piece of paper out of your pocket. *Secrets of the Ya-Ya Sisterhood*, it says. Oh great, you think. You wait for the Blockbuster clerk to complete ringing up the customer standing in front of you, whom the clerk refers to as François—a high-school-aged, athletic-looking kid wearing a golf shirt, whose extended right hand is disappearing and reappearing as it gracefully slides back and forth in the lower center region of the buttocks of the woman standing really close to him, who, although she bears no resemblance, is old enough to be his mother. When the transaction is completed, François turns to the woman, without losing his hand placement or interrupting its rhythmic movement, and says, "Come on, Christine, let's go." They do.

You ask the clerk, as quietly as possible, where *Secrets of the Ya-Ya Sisterhood* is while looking at the paper your wife handed you, so that he, and anyone else listening, knows that this is not your selection but your wife's.

He smiles, because he is familiar with this scene, as he points to the Drama section. It's over in the Drama section, under *S*, about three-quarters of the way down that aisle. You head over that way. You arrive at the section and there are eight boxes of this movie, but, to your surprise, they all seem to be checked out. You now have to go through the embarrassment of going back to the clerk, waiting for him to finish with the customers who are waiting in line ahead of you, and asking him if there are any available copies of this movie elsewhere in the store. You wait in line impatiently.

Finally it is your turn. He looks up and recognizes you.

"Find it?" he asks, smiling, to which you respond that all the copies were checked out. He bangs on his keyboard, hits return a few times, looks up at you, and says, louder than you wished, "Sorry, all copies of *Secrets of the Ya-Ya Sisterhood* are checked out." This is the best news that you have received all day long and you want to tip this Blockbuster clerk, but you don't.

You rushed out of the house and forgot your phone, so, oh well, you cannot call your wife to ask her for another one of her selections. The ball is in your court now. You fall back into your old habits and begin with *A*s in the New Release section. You look at every film that looks remotely appealing and read each description. You make mental notes of the ones that sound good to return to after you have done your tour of duty. As you make your rounds, you know that your fallback is *Day of the Jackal*; you recently read the book and loved it.

A half hour slips by, and you are suddenly cognizant of the time. You ask the clerk, with more confidence and volume in your voice than before, where you would find *Day of the Jackal*, and he looks at you approvingly, as if he notices that you had just found the penis that you lost when you first arrived at the store. He tells you to look over in Suspense, under *D*. This is a movie that you convince yourself your wife will love and think is a great substitute for *Secrets of the Ya-Ya Sisterhood*. You know that it will also make her happy knowing that you are watching something that you find enjoyable.

You find the movie and it hasn't been checked out. You wait in line for the three people in front of you to check out, a process that takes five minutes per person, then you check out and go home.

You arrive excitedly opening the back door and your wife is at the kitchen table with a bunch of papers strewn about her. "Hi, honey," you say. "Where were you? Why did you take so long?" she asks accusingly. "Well, *Secrets of the Ya-Ya Sisterhood* was completely checked out and I had to select another movie. I got *Day of the Jackal*. You will love this movie," you add.

You know instantly by your wife's reaction that *Day of the Jackal* is not on her must-see list and that she is disappointed. "Why didn't you call me for another movie suggestion?" she asks. You tell her that you forgot your phone and she looks at you suspiciously. "Did you remember to get the milk?" she asks. You did not. She tells you to go down and put the movie on and that she will be down in a minute.

You go downstairs, to the basement, where you have put the TV in your house so that it is inconvenient for your kids to watch it, and you insert the DVD into your new piece of hardware. The movie comes on and you realize, ten minutes into it, that it is looking familiar. You realize that this is not because you have just read the book. You assume that you saw it on a plane on one of your business trips, because if your wife had seen it she would have been so kind as to tell you the minute that you excitedly told her of your selection, the one that you chose with her in mind.

You are a half hour into the movie and your wife still has not arrived. You pause the film and go up to the kitchen. She is gone. You realize that she went up to bed.

You finish watching the movie, all alone, knowing everything that has happened. You go to bed and your wife is sleeping. You do not have sex that night, like you may have if you had brought home a movie that was on Robin's list.

YOUR
SUBURBAN
SPRING

Draft a Little League Baseball Team

More than anything, you love doing things with your kids, especially playing sports. You played sports growing up and you have always been OK. Not great, but not so bad, either. But now it is a whole different story. There is nothing like playing a sport with a group of eight-year-olds to make you feel more athletic than you have ever felt in your life. You are in your athletic prime.

Your suburb takes its baseball seriously. You assembled a team of first-graders last year in a coaches-pitch baseball league. The team consisted of your kid and his friends, and because you knew where and how to pitch to each kid on your team, they were all hitters. You attempt to import your last year's team into the second-grade league, and after trying everything you can think of you cannot do it. You look upon yourself as someone who can convince anyone to do anything, a skill that you have perfected as a corporate executive, but is useless in this Little League.

There are tryouts in this league, which are called "evaluations," coupled with a draft. The reason for this is to assure that the teams are evenly balanced, although you know that some of the other coaches have figured out the loopholes so that they could stack their teams. You have not made the effort to investigate any loopholes in the system because your only motivation is to try to keep friends together. You show up for the draft. The setting is this: there is one manager and three coaches for each of the twenty-four teams in the league—ninety-six dads who sit in prearranged seating in a gym set back along the first- and third-base lines of a painted baseball diamond. Each coach is given a clipboard and evaluation forms to assess the performance of each of the 336 second-grade kids who signed up for baseball that year. You are given a pencil to record your comments and your scores, which are to be tallied after the evaluations so that you can rank each of these 336 second-graders, in order of best to worst (from 1 to 336). Each kid gets to come into this lair of coaches, alone, with an identifying number pinned to the back of his shirt, and shows the ninety-six coaches and managers how he hits, throws, catches, and runs.

One by one, each kid enters the coaches' lair and tries his best, for the most part. Except for the six kids who wish they were anywhere but here. Those six kids are on each of the ninety-six coaches' and managers' special list of kids not to choose for their team, no matter what.

After this fun-filled activity, you lag behind with your coach friends and rank each of the kids and assemble your strategy for the draft. The other managers and coaches do the same.

On Tuesday evening, you and the other ninety-six managers and coaches show up at a recreation-center meeting room to select your teams. This is the draft. You have your preranked list and so have they. The manager for each team then selects a number out of a hat, to determine their order in the draft.

The draft commences and each team selects one player per turn, moving down their list of ranked players. The players are identified only by the numbers that were pinned to their backs during the "evaluation." When a player is selected, you and all the other managers cross the player off your lists. Throughout this process, you are surprised by the consistency with which the players have been ranked by all the managers and coaches.

This process is moving along with a high degree of predictability, with one exception. You notice your friend Stephen, a manager for a competing team, is making draft selections that are entirely inconsistent with the way in which you and every other manager and coach in the room has ranked the players. For instance, for his first pick he selects the player that you ranked number 94 on your list. His next selection was some kid who was number 114 on your list, and his third draft pick was number 67 on your list. Each and every one of his subsequent selections seems equally illogical. Each time Stephen makes a selection, the other managers and coaches in the room laugh. You do not, because you know three things about Stephen:

1. He has older sons and has been through this before.
2. He is funny.
3. He is smart.

The draft concludes and you have assembled a respectable team. You do not get a chance to talk with Stephen before he leaves to see what he was doing. However, you get a much better idea of Stephen's draft strategy when you arrive for your first game against his team. On his sidelines spectating the game are fourteen of the most attractive moms, excluding your kids' mom, who reside in your suburb. Many you have seen before with glowing hair at the black-light bowling alley. Stephen, having been a coach for one of his older sons a few years ago, knows that with three practices and two games a week the fans are an important part of assembling a team. You win the game 14–1. Stephen's team becomes each manager's and player's favorite opposing team.

Listen to a Guy Tell You How Great His Kids Are

You live in a suburb where all of the kids are active and involved in many activities from a very young age. They all play many sports, they all have academic interests, they all can navigate a computer more capably than most of the adults that live in your suburb, and they are all exposed to movies and a wide range of cultural events.

Because of the broad exposure that all of these fortunate kids experience, parents have generally learned not to be obnoxious in talking with their friends about how wonderful their kids are or how many character-building activities their kids are involved in. They have learned this because they realize that everyone's kids are in overdrive with these activities and that almost nothing is unique and that people just don't want to hear about it.

It is nine o'clock on a Saturday morning and you are at your daughter's preschool's open house. You enter the school and the first thing that you do is sit down at a preschool-size round table in a chair whose seat is as high as the midpoint between your ankle and your knee. You sit down there with your daughter at this small table in the hallway, outside of her classroom. You are eating this wonderful coffee cake that your daughter has been telling you that she and her classmates made yesterday; it is coffee cake without coffee, she has told you three times that morning, and you are raving about it to her. You tell her that it is the best coffee cake that you have ever eaten, and you are probably fairly accurate, because coffee cake has never been high on your list of favorite foods.

You are enjoying your coffee cake with your daughter while seated in the world's smallest chair at the world's lowest table. In the middle of her wonderfully expressive coffee-cake story, another dad, whom you have never met, joins you with his daughter, a girl that your daughter does not know. As he sits down, and before he says hello to you or your daughter, he says, while interrupting your daughter's coffee-cake story, that, while it is only 9:15 A.M. on this Saturday, he has already been to a basketball game for one of his sons and a swim meet for his daughter. Here is your interpretation of what was really said and the conversation that his comment prompted.

What he said: "I can't believe that it is 9:15 A.M. on Saturday and I have already been to my son's basketball game and my daughter's swim meet."

What you think he meant: I am Super Dad, probably better than you, waking up so early on a Saturday morning to see my kids play sports, and I am grooming my kids to be great athletes. I bet you did not take any of your kids to any sporting activities this morning, like I did. My kids are better than yours, they are more active than yours, and I am an amazing dad who has an amazing wife for scheduling my kids into such wholesome activities. In fact, I am probably a better athlete than you.

What you think about what he said: You are an asshole. Didn't you read the memo, the one that says that you should not brag about your kids and never interrupt a kid when she is excitedly expressing a constructive thought?

How you would respond if you were like him: So, big deal, I am not impressed. My daughter swims at 10 A.M., then goes to climbing class at 11. My son has a basketball game at 11, right after his swim lesson with Annika; a pinewood-derby race at 2 and tennis at 4 P.M. I coach my kid's football and baseball teams and am my son's Cub Scout den leader. I spend more time with my kids and do more stuff with them than you probably ever will. And, besides, I am in my athletic prime. You are nothing special. I just know better than to brag about all this, because every kid who lives in this suburb is involved in so many things that none of it is impressive to anyone. No one really cares.

What you actually say in response: "Come on, honey, show me your classroom now. That was the best coffee cake I have ever had."

Total a Car

A bigger shot than you moves from the city into a house around the corner. At least, you think that he is a bigger shot than you, because he has a bright-red Ferrari. You heard that this car costs $250,000. It could be that he is not such a big deal, because instead of investing in real estate with a dad whom he met on the sidelines of his kid's soccer game, who, like you, has a vowel on the end of his last name, he bought a bright-red, $250,000 Ferrari, which you guess has been fed nothing but premium gasoline. That is what you tell yourself, anyway.

The curious thing is that the seven-figure house that this Italian sports-car aficionado has purchased has no garage. So the Ferrari gets parked on the street, which is irritating to some. It is an odd contrast to the brick street upon which it is parked and the old homes that look out over it. If it were parked on your street, your son would feel an immediate urge to play baseball with a brand-new hardball on the front lawn.

Four years before Ferrari guy moved into your neighborhood, your village redid the entire sewer system to rectify a problem. The problem then was that when it rained hard the rainwater would quickly drain into the sewer pipes that ran underneath the nice brick streets. The sewer pipes would get overfilled and the rainwater that was in the sewer pipe, which would get mixed in with toilet water, had nowhere to go except to back up into the pipes that connected the homes in your suburb to the sewer system. The overflowing water would then end up in everyone's basement. Stinky and no fun at all.

One year, the village decided to tap into some of its $60-million-a-year tax revenues and put restrictor valves on the sewer drains. Restrictor valves are like big funnels that regulate the rate at which rainwater flows into the sewer system, basically slowing it. As a result, the water no longer backs up into anyone's basement. However, the by-product of this sewer upgrade is that water stays in the streets longer. In fact, when it rains hard, as it does a few times a year, water rises to one, two, or even three feet in the low spots along your suburban streets. It may take four or five hours for the water to drain through the restrictor valves and into the sewer system to a point where the streets are puddle-free.

One evening, exactly four days after moving into his new overpriced home without a garage, your new neighbor, the trader, parked his low-slung, bright-red, $250,000, premium-gasoline-filled Ferrari in the lowest spot along the brick street in front of his charming old house. The spot that he chose is in a little valley with a slight rise in front of and to the rear of the Ferrari. To your new neighbor, it appears to be the perfect spot, as the driver's door of the car is directly adjacent to the walkway of his new home's front door. There is no better and more convenient place to park, or so he thought that evening.

That night, it rains like a mother. You wake up the next morning and are out of your house at 4:45 A.M. to take a limo to pick up your friend-boss and then head to the airport. You put on a pair of boots and walk to the limo, which is parked in

140

front of your house, which is sitting in a foot of water. You can see that the restrictor valves have done their job that night, just as they were designed to do. There is plenty of water in the street, and none in anyone's basements.

You direct the limo driver to carefully stay on flat streets that will be less flooded than the streets with bumps. You avoid any streets where there are low spots. When making a left-hand turn onto Orchard Street, you pass by Ginkgo Street and notice the red roof of what looks like your new neighbor's red Ferrari. It is. You cannot see any other part of the car, because, except for about five inches of its roof, the entire car is underwater.

That is the last time you ever see the red Ferrari. A month later, a black one shows up and it is parked on the *rise* in the street.

Bring the Kids to the Auto-Recycling Facility
with Their Friends

You are at the school benefit for your daughter's preschool, which your wife has organized. You "win" a few things at this auction. You hear people use this term "win" at this auction, but what you are really winning is the right to pay more than anyone else would possibly think of paying for an item you do not need. You call that losing, not winning.

One thing that you have "won" at this auction is a "tour of an auto-recycling facility" for five kids and their parents. You have won the right to pay $250 for this because absolutely nobody bid against you. You are drawn to this item because you imagine it to be a huge facility that melts down metal or whatever it is that is done to recycle autos. You have been on factory tours before; you have been to Ben & Jerry's to see how ice cream is made, to the Coors Brewery to see how beer is made, and to Ethan Allen, where you watched furniture makers turn canopy-bed posts. You expect the tour of the auto-recycling facility to be very similar to the other tours you have been on. They are well organized and professionally run, with fun take-homes for the kids when you leave. A lot of these tours are sanitized, insulating you from what really goes on, but despite that it should still be a fun outing.

At this auction, like many of the neighborhood-oriented auctions you attend, you will experience, as you have come to expect, seeing some of your neighbors involved in brutal bidding wars. They will compete with one another to "win," and when they "win" they will have won the right to pay $6,000 for their kid and three of her friends to have a sleepover at the school with her teacher. Some overachieving bidder will "win" the privilege of paying $7,500 to play a round of golf in North Carolina (transportation *not* included), and another neighbor will "win" the $10,000 guitar that Bruce Springsteen supposedly played once in New Jersey. The "winners" are competing with their kids' schoolmates' parents (their neighbors) to see who can wake up tomorrow morning and feel like the biggest loser.

For the tour of the auto-recycling plant that you have "won," you call up five of your kids' friends' parents and you get five easy yeses. Nobody asks for details, and that is a good thing, because the yeses may not have come so easily had your kids' five friends' parents asked a basic question, like where the facility was located.

The Friday before the Saturday you scheduled the tour, you get the address, which is on Ninety-fifth Street in the city, a neighborhood with which most of your kids' friends' parents are unfamiliar, because it is on the deep South Side of Chicago. It is a neighborhood that many people in your suburb have paid handsomely to move as far away from as possible. You call your kids' friends' parents with the address, an address that everyone recognizes as being on the South Side, but where few of them have ever been. At this point, those five quick yeses are all wishing they hadn't said yes so quickly. It is too late to back out now. Most of what everyone has heard about the South Side has to do with gangs, housing projects, drive-by shootings, crime, and poverty. It would be awkward to back out now, because everyone has already said yes.

You tell them that it is OK, it will be safe. "It is Ninety-fifth Street," you say. "Ninety-fifth Street is busy and there is nothing to worry about." Not that you know any of this, but you think that this "auto-recycling facility" will be a memorable experience that they would never have had otherwise, plus you want some company for you and your kid. "We will all be better off having seen this auto-recycling plant," you say. "It will be a great experience for the kids." You have just barely convinced your kids' friends' parents, who you can tell have all become suspicious of your parental judgment during these phone conversations. You get the impression that they would much rather be embracing diversity in your suburb, where there is none, than on the South Side of Chicago.

That Saturday morning, you load your kid into the car and start heading south. This will be a great family outing, you think. You have always wondered how cars are recycled. You arrive at Ninety-fifth Street and it narrows into a small street. On this street in this neighborhood, unlike yours, you will politely pull over to the side of the street when an opposing car is coming your way. You do not want to give anyone in this neighborhood any reason to get angry with you. It is quiet and desolate. You are expecting a big building with smokestacks and a large asphalt parking lot with a designated visitors' section. You are expecting that there will be men in white jumpsuits manipulating car-recycling controls. You expect that you will be directed to a viewing area behind some heavy-duty glass listening to a recorded tour or be escorted by an attractive, professional tour guide, like the woman who gave you and your family a tour of Ben & Jerry's in Vermont.

As you pull up to this address, you are puzzled, because there is none of this. There is a beaten-up trailer sitting on wheels that are fully deflated. The rusted and dented trailer looks like someone may be living in it. There is a weathered wooden fence, which in some sections is still standing. There is no parking lot. There is no specially marked "Visitors Park Here" section. You park on the street near the trailer. You are the first to arrive and you hope that your premium-gasoline-fueled German luxury vehicle will not go through some recycling of its own in the time that it takes you to tour this "facility." You hesitantly approach the trailer and the door opens before you arrive. "Hi, I'm Tonya," a friendly voice yells out. "Welcome to our auto-recycling facility."

You introduce yourself and your family and let Tonya know that you are the first to arrive. Over the next fifteen minutes, your kids' friends and families gather, each one as curious as you about what condition their European cars will be in when they return from this "facility" tour, for which you are responsible. They, like you, are probably wondering where the "facility" is, because the only thing that looks at all like a facility is the beat-up trailer that Tonya walked out of fifteen minutes ago. No one is smiling and no one has thanked you for inviting them.

Tonya assembles the group and tells everyone to follow her into the recycling facility, which to you looks like something that you would call a junkyard. The "recycling facility" is a lot the size of half a football field. Covering the ground are metal scraps, glass shards, car parts, doors, engines, engine parts, transmissions, lots of oil and grease, and some stripped-out car shells that are strewn about but that appear to be ready to be "recycled." Tonya explains to all of the kids how they get the cars, strip off all the parts that can be resold, then crush what is left of the cars, to be hauled away and melted. She asks who would like to crush a car and five hands instantly shoot up.

On her walkie-talkie, she calls the forklift operator, Jim. The arrangement is this, Tonya explains. Each kid will drive with Jim in the forklift. With Jim, each kid will select a car that they want to bring over to the hydraulic press. With Jim, they will insert the car into the press, sandwich it between two massive slabs of steel, get out of the forklift truck, and press the two buttons on the hydraulic press, which sets the top slab into an unstoppable downward motion, crushing the car shell.

"Who would like to go first?" Tonya asks. Five hands shoot up, more quickly than before. Jim pulls around in the forklift and takes the first kid. They do just as Tonya described. Over the next hour and a half, five kids have crushed five car shells as flat as a pancake.

You leave wondering what your car is looking like and you are relieved to know that it is just as you left it, as are your friends' cars. Your friends thank you profusely for inviting them on this outing, a facility tour that they will never, ever forget.

You leave Tonya knowing that you will never "win" anything cooler at any school benefit in your life.

Teach Your Son About Sex

Your son is in second grade and you are in New York City on a business trip with your friend-boss and two other colleagues. You have left for New York on a Monday and are planning to return Tuesday evening.

You have not thought yet about having any discussions with your children about sex, because you think that they are just way too young. You, for instance, have never discussed this topic with your parents, nor do you think that you have even said the word "sex" around them in the forty-four years of your life. Growing up, you would have never even considered asking either of your parents about sex. Why would you? With Billy Semitini's *Playboy* stash, who needed to ask their parents anything?

You and your wife have a much different relationship with your kids than you had with your parents. You are both very open with them and there are really no topics that are off limits in your house. In this regard, your household is much more like the household that your wife grew up in than yours. You and your wife agree on this, like you agree on many core philosophical issues. You and your wife even have almost the exact same tastes in houses and artwork, in that you can predict with great accuracy what she will like in art and houses and that her preferences in both will be entirely in line with yours.

You call home on Tuesday morning, after you and your friend–boss have taken a run in Central Park, showered, gotten dressed, and eaten an overpriced breakfast at the Essex House, one of your preferred hotels in New York, because it is close to Central Park and to the New York Athletic Club.

You are standing in the lobby waiting for your small group of four to gather, and while you have a minute of downtime you figure out a way to fill it, another trait that has been passed along to you from prior generations. You call your wife. "Hi, honey, how is everything going? I am just calling to check in," you say. "Well, everything is going OK, but you won't believe the conversation that Blake and I had this morning." You love to hear about your son's discussions and you ask your wife, excitedly, what they were talking about.

"Blake asked me where babies come from," your wife says. "What did you tell him?" you ask curiously. "Well," she said, "I read an article that I think was in this week's issue of *People.*" "*People* magazine?" you ask, astounded that anyone with a college degree would cite that publication as an authority on any topic. "What do you think I meant?" she responds back. "Sorry, honey, I wasn't thinking."

"Well, this article in *People* indicated that if your child is inquiring about sex you should be straightforward with them and give them enough information to satisfy their curiosity. You do not want to erode your credibility with your kids," she says authoritatively.

At this point, you wonder how much curiosity your son had and how extensively your wife satisfied it, and to what extent she did not erode her credibility with your once-innocent son. "So what did you tell him?" you ask, accepting the fact that there is absolutely nothing you could possibly do to turn around this series of surprisingly premature events. "Well, I did what the article said," she says. "And how did you interpret that article?" you ask, expecting the worst at this point.

"Well, I told him that Mommy and Daddy hug in a special way, and when we do we make a baby." That sounds pretty good, you think to yourself. "What do you mean 'a special way'?" Your wife goes on telling you of your son's response to her explanation. "Well," your wife goes on further, to do her best to abide by the authorities on this topic that *People* magazine has endorsed, "Daddy puts his penis into Mommy's vagina and then Mommy gets pregnant and has a baby."

You could imagine your son at this point in the conversation, which took place an hour earlier, listening more attentively than he has ever listened to anything in his entire life.

"You told him that?" you ask. "Yes, I wanted to be honest with him. But I did a really smart thing," she adds. "I told him not to tell any of his friends, in case their parents do not want them to know about sex at this age." "Good call," you say. "Was that in the *People* article, too?" you add sarcastically.

Your three colleagues are assembled in the hotel lobby at this point and they are ready to go. "Honey," you say, "nice job with being open and forthcoming. I have to go now. I love you." She concludes the conversation, saying proudly, "Mark, the eagle has landed."

You hang up and your friend-boss asks what is going on. You tell him that you left your son yesterday a boy, and that you will return to him tonight a man.

You arrive home that evening and you greet your wife and daughter, who are in the kitchen. "Where is Blake, the man?" you ask, inquiring as to the whereabouts of your second-grade boy. "He is upstairs in his room reading."

You go upstairs to greet your son and to make sure that he

has not grown a beard or something since you saw him last. "What are you reading?" you ask him. "A book that Mommy got for me at the library." You look at the title, which you re-call as *My Body and Me*, and your son has the book opened to the page where a cartoon drawing of a naked girl is in front of him with call-out captions describing the various features that your wife had, earlier that day, articulated to him with great clarity. He smiles at you and you run downstairs.

"Why did you get that book for Blake? Wasn't your conver-sation with him graphic enough?" you ask. She tells you that the *People* article said that you should get age-appropriate books that the kids can understand to reinforce discussions you may have with them about sex.

That night, when you are putting your son to bed, he asks you, just after you finished saying a prayer (a Catholic one) with him and as you are about to leave his room, "Daddy, can you and Mommy show me how you hug in that special way?"

YOUR SUBURBAN SUMMER

Go to the Beach

You live a few blocks from the lake. In fact, you paid more than anyone would guess for your house because it is so close to the beach, one of the nicest beaches around, and you try to go to the beach as often as possible all year round. One day, when you were in Santa Monica, you even told your friend-boss and a colleague that you thought your beach was nicer than the Santa Monica beach, and you meant it. They laughed at you.

School ends and you go to the beach with your family one Saturday. Your son has just completed his first year of Spanish with Mrs. . . . well, you are not quite so sure what her last name is, because after an entire year of Spanish your son admits to you that he has no idea what her name is. You cannot believe this and it disturbs you. "How can you not know your teacher's name after spending an entire year with her?" you ask disappointedly, a question to which you will get no response that you can understand.

While you have never met your son's Spanish teacher, your son has pointed her out to you on two occasions, and one thing you do know about her is that she did not grow up in some white-bread suburb, like you and many of the people you know. How do you know that? Well, for one, she has an accent. Second, she is exotic-looking. You have noticed her at the kids' soccer games, and, come to think of it, so has every other dad. She wears skin-tight clothes all the time. She has long black curly hair and a perpetual golden tan. In your mind, she is from Buenos Aires, Rio de Janeiro, or somewhere where people seem wonderfully exotic to you, are not afraid to wear skin-tight clothes, and speak English with wonderful accents. Each time you see her, the song "Girl from Ipanema" pops into your head. She is tall and tan and young and lovely, and, like a samba, she sways so gently when she walks. You have also heard a lot of "ahhhh"s as she goes walking by. You know your son's other teachers by name, but not his Spanish teacher. You head down to the beach that Saturday afternoon. You approach the gated area, where a high-school kid, who has scored the best summer job there is, is supposed to check your beach pass. The relaxed pass checker is sitting in a chair under a large sun umbrella and does not acknowledge you or your pass, except to say "Cool" as you walk by. You walk past him, assuming that means that you are OK to do so. You are sure that he lets anyone go into your suburb's restricted beach, which you are paying the highest taxes in the country to enjoy.

As you enter the beach, you visually scan the shorefront for a place to set up. Your son, horrified, tells you that he sees his Spanish teacher. You are impressed with his observational skills; from where you are standing, the shore is at least seventy-five yards away and many, many people are standing there. You are amazed that your son is able to identify his Spanish teacher out of the huge crowd.

"Where is she?" you ask somewhat curiously, because you are interested in knowing the people who are influencing your child when you are absent. "There she is," he says. "She is the one standing up." You look to try to identify a woman who is standing up and you realize that half of the three hundred women at the beach on this first hot day after school has been let out are standing up. His clue does not help you. "Blake," you say, "there are at least a hundred women standing up by the water. Could you be a little more vague, please?" He laughs at your request and says, "Are you blind, Dad? She is the lady with her butt sticking out."

Sure enough, among more than three hundred women enjoying the beach on that Saturday, there is one who is different from all the others. She is wearing a bathing suit that you are sure was not purchased anywhere in your suburb. It is a bathing suit that is not the kind that conceals one's butt. It is a very nice bathing suit, you think, one that you wished more women, a select group, who patronize your beach would embrace. It is a bathing suit, you notice, with one little strap, you imagine—because you cannot really see it—a little wider than the width of kite string, that seems to disappear somewhere in her buttocks. It reappears when it attaches to another string, about the same size, which encircles her waist. You detect another two straps of the same dimension, one going around her back, the other disappearing behind her long flowing dark hair. You are amazed at your son's power of observation and, at this point, yours. You and all the other dads on the beach today will set a new suburban standard in embracing diversity.

"So, that is your Spanish teacher?" you ask, becoming more interested in your son's foreign-language studies than you have ever been. "Yes, that's her." At this point, she has turned around to reveal a tiny equilateral-triangle patch that covers a small but important section of her frontal region, well below her navel, that you assume to be attached to the kite-like string that has disappeared into her buttocks. There are two similar triangular patches, about the same size, which you can only describe as tiny, concealing a small portion of her ample, well-rounded breasts.

"Blake," you say, "could you please introduce Mommy and Daddy to your Spanish teacher? What is her name?" you ask. "I have no idea, Dad," he responds. You remember that your son does not know her name and again you are appalled that he spent two mornings a week for the entire school year with this woman in a classroom of eleven kids and has no idea what her name is. It is unlike him, as he is usually very good with names and frequently helps you out with recalling a name that you have forgotten.

Excited to share his academic interests with his parents, your son escorts you over to this woman, after you force him to do so against his will. You are with your son, your daughter, and your wife and you are excitedly on your way to meet your son's Spanish teacher. All of your neighbors will be so impressed with how interested and involved you and your family are in your son's schooling when they see you engaged in a discussion with her on the beach.

You are now within talking distance of your son's Spanish teacher and she sees your son. "Roberto!" she exclaims. "¿Como estas?" Your son, whose field of vision at this point is about parallel with his Spanish teacher's lowest triangular patch, cannot think of a suitable response to this foreign-language question in any language. You decide to pitch in and help him out. "Estoy muy, muy bien," you say, speaking better Spanish now than you ever have in your entire life.

Lucky you and your family talk with her for a few minutes after she introduces herself to your entire family as Reneta Quesadda. What a memorable name, you think. How could your son, or anyone else, for that matter, not remember that? What is wrong with your kid? you think. She tells you that she has enjoyed having your son, Roberto, which you think is an unusual derivative of Blake, in her class. You respond, "Not as much as he enjoyed having you as a teacher," but you are thinking, Not as much as I am enjoying standing before you right now.

During your conversation, you have difficulty maintaining eye contact with your son's Spanish teacher, as does everyone on the beach. You are severely distracted by three undersized triangular patches and a few disappearing and reappearing kite strings. This suit, you think, is an engineering marvel. Before leaving, his teacher makes your son sing a little Spanish song with her, where at the end she gestures to him by thrusting her lower triangular patch toward him a few times while clenching her outstretched fists and pulling them toward her. While your son is horrified that he was made to do this little song with his teacher, who is thrusting her pelvic region at him while standing on the beach, you are more motivated now to learn Spanish than you have ever been in your entire life and ask if she could teach you the song. At which point your wife indicates to you that you had better go now. "We are meeting the Millers," she tells you, a fact that you were not aware of until now, "and we are running late." You give your son's Spanish teacher a big adios, and as you are walking over to meet your friends your son asks, "Dad, what did my Spanish teacher say her name is?" "I have no idea, Roberto," you respond.

Go Kayaking

You have a friend, Bob Lauter, who organizes treks to the North Pole and Antarctica for a living and who also arranges two-week-long kayak trips from Greek island to Greek island. Locally, he teaches classes using his own kayaks, and he has a lot of them. He frequently brings his kayaks to your beach in the summer, transporting them on large, specially made trailers. You think how you can use his skills and his toys to your benefit.

His kid and your kid play together. You invite his son, who, by the way, at two years of age was the youngest person ever to travel to the North Pole, to be in your Cub Scout den.

Throughout the year, your den engages in various activities that the dads arrange. Your den is a dads' den, which is different from when you were a Cub Scout. When you were a Cub Scout, moms ran the show, and you made Popsicle-stick birdhouses and stuff like that. Not your den. Your den goes rock climbing, gets behind-the-scenes airport tours, goes on long hikes, swims, plays dodgeball, goes on bike rides, builds and launches model rockets, goes on fishing expeditions, goes sailing and kayaking—stuff like that. The dads' activities are all good, and there is pressure on each dad to come up with something that will outdo what other dads come up with, because, you all realize, you are in competition with one another, even though it is Cub Scouts, no one will ever acknowledge that fact.

Summer is approaching, and you ask your Antarctic traveler friend if he would be so kind as to coordinate a kayak trip for the kids. Without hesitation, he says yes. You cannot believe that you have a guy like this in your kids' life. You and your den are very fortunate. You agree to meet at the beach, and when you arrive you notice that there are more people there than are in your den. These are all people who live in your suburb and this outing will be even more fun than you thought.

Your real-estate partner, Joe Sclafanni, shows up with his kid. They are not in Cub Scouts. Joe is one of your best friends; you talk once or twice a day and you laugh together about the problems that you have to deal with in your buildings and the personalities of your tenants. You get into a blue kayak that your son selects, because blue is his favorite color, and your friend Joe and his son select a green kayak based on the same principle. There are thirty or so people occupying twenty or so kayaks, and two instructors. One instructor will take the "advanced" group, the group where you and your son place yourselves, because you have gone kayaking before. Your friend Joe and his son join the "advanced" group as well, along with a few others who perceive themselves to be advanced. The word "advanced" scares many away from joining your group, because, compared with your guide, who for the past twenty years of his life has been taking groups of adventurers for month-long kayak trips in the Mediterranean Sea, you are all beginners. The difference between one group and the other is more a function of how the participants perceive themselves than anything to do with skill level. Of one thing you are sure:

anyone with a vowel on the end of their last name will end up in the "advanced" group.

Your "advanced" group starts off. Your mission is to paddle to the next suburb to the north, the suburb where your friend-boss lives, the one where the median values of homes are $400,000 higher than in the suburb where you live. You look forward to seeing how the richest neighbors of yours spend Saturdays at their beach.

You and your friend and your respective kids are paddling along. It is relaxed and it is fun. Before you know it, the pace picks up a bit. Not that either you or your friend initiate the quickened pace. It just seems to happen. Within a hundred yards of the launch, you are paddling as hard as you can. Your son asks you to slow down but you do not. Your friend Joe's son asks him the same question and his son gets the same response that your son has just gotten: "Paddle faster."

What has happened is the inevitable: you are in a race. You have not articulated that thought, nor has your son. Neither has your friend or his son. But everyone knows it. You know that he knows that you are in a race, because he, like you, has a vowel on the end of his last name. Having a vowel strategically located as the last letter of your last name means that many things you do turn into a competition, even though others around you rarely see it that way. Like many things, because you are a man, and because you have a vowel at the end of your last name, there is no reason to talk about this recent development, this two-kayak race you are in.

You and your son are going all out. So are they. You know your destination because it has been called out by your instructor when your advanced group first assembled. It is a long way off. This is a distance race. Pace yourself, you think.

Your son slacks off a bit, and you "encourage" him as best you can. You remember that you are on a Cub Scout outing and this is supposed to bring you closer to your son and his friends. As the den leader, you should be setting the example. You should be exemplifying courteous, kind, cheerful, and reverent. You know this in your head, but you do not have time for example setting and bonding, because you are in a race and the outcome of this race will determine something more important than setting an example.

You paddle furiously and do not have the extra breath to talk with your son or your friends. You get to the finish line just one boat length behind your friend and his son. You are all sweating and your arms are sore and tired. "That was great," your friend says, turning around to acknowledge that he is the winner. "Yeah," you say, "that is a great arm workout," meaning, but not saying, that your arms are spent.

"It's such a great day, isn't it?" your friend says, meaning, but not saying, "We beat you by a boat length, therefore we are better kayakers than you." "Yeah," you say. "What a relaxing way to spend the afternoon," meaning, "There is no way that I will ever admit to this guy that I am tired, even though I could not pick up a fork right now if I had to."

You all jump out of your kayaks into the water and swim. You pull your kayaks up onto the beach. You wait for the others to arrive. You wait for a long time. When they are in sight, you yell out to everyone, "Hey, you guys, isn't this great?" meaning, "We beat you, you are not as fast as us." They agree, knowing what you mean, because they have no alternative. "Yes, we had a nice relaxing paddle over here," meaning, "You guys are assholes for racing against each other."

Open the Windows

You frequently drive with your wife and kids, and whenever you do you are the driver. You are a driver who likes to drive with the windows open, especially in the summer on days when it is eighty degrees out. Even on very hot days, you like to crank up the AC and open the windows. There is something about fresh air that you really enjoy. It is one of those small pleasures in life that makes you very happy.

Unlike you, your wife does not seem to enjoy the feeling of air washing over her while driving, and she has a very subtle way of revealing that fact to you. She closes the windows immediately after detecting that they are open, usually starting with your window. It could be a beautiful, eighty-five-degree day and an open window will really bother her. She will reach to the center console, where the window controls are located, and proceed to close your window first, because that is the open window that seems to bother her the most. Then she will close her window, followed by the back windows. She thinks that because the fresh air annoys her it is as annoying to everyone else in the car.

What is especially bothersome to her, for reasons that you

are unclear of, is an open sunroof. You are lucky enough to have two sunroofs in your SUV, which influenced your decision to buy the overpriced gas-guzzler, but neither will get to be opened for more than a minute or two because it takes only that long until you detect your wife's left hand reaching for the overhead, roof-mounted sunroof controls. Sometimes you will try to sneak open a sunroof, say, before your wife gets in the car while you are waiting in it for her, but every time she will notice that it is open and it will bother her. When she does notice, she will look at you like you have done the most ridiculous thing imaginable as she depresses the rocker switch, closing it.

You cannot begin to understand why she would want those windows and sunroofs closed, but she does. It becomes her top priority each time you and she are in the car together. One hypothesis that you have going, but which you have never shared with her, is that she knows you get great pleasure out of driving with open windows and sunroofs, just like you get pleasure from drinking grape juice, and that is pleasure she does not want you to have. Often she will call you from home while you are in the car on your cell phone and will tell you that she cannot hear you because the window is open. You close it. An open car window annoys her even when she is not in the car.

But one day you drive your friend-boss's car home. It is a Volvo convertible and you drive home with the top down. You pull up to the front of the house and the kids announce to Mom that "Dad got a convertible." Your wife comes to greet you as you are walking up to the house, knowing that the car belongs to your friend-boss, and looks at the car enviously. "I love convertibles. Can't we get one?" she says.

Go Windsurfing

One thing that you like to do at the beach is windsurf. To windsurf, you launch from the sailing beach, a beach reserved for boaters, not swimmers. It is a hot day and you call your friends and tell them to meet you at the beach. You tell them that you have a great idea. "We will meet you down at the north end of the sailing beach," you tell them. "The kids will have a great time swimming there and I will bring my windsurfer down so that the kids can surf on it and dive off of it." This will be a fun beach day. You get your suits on, round up all the beach gear, and everyone piles in the car for the three-minute ride.

To the south is the swimming beach for your suburb's residents only, and to the immediate north of that is the sailing beach, also exclusively for the residents of your suburb. To the north of the sailing beach is a private stretch of beach that serves as the enormous sandy backyards of your suburb's nine most expensive homes. The private beach, you assume, is for the exclusive use of the nine homeowners who have paid for this privilege. Their homes are all eight-digit homes and most of the forty- to fifty-year-old dads who live in these homes, you assume, have received enormous sums of money for cashing out of something or other and for the most part wear shorts, T-shirts, and sandals when they go to "work" every day. You do not make eye contact with those homes, because they are a constant reminder to you that you are not winning this particular competition, not yet, anyway.

The private beach is important to you because it is adjacent to the section of the sailing beach that has been delegated for windsurfers. You figure that on this Saturday everyone in your small group, even you, will get to do exactly what they want to at the beach. You will go windsurfing while your kids just step over the imaginary line in the water and go swimming in the private-beach water. When you come in with your windsurfer, you will pop off the sail and your kids can mess around on it and use it as a surfboard/diving board. Perfect!

You unload your wife, the kids, towels, sand toys, beach bags, football, Frisbee, lacrosse sticks, and life vests and head off to park the car. You wave to your friends, who have already done the same, and your wife and kids go to join them. You go park your car in the lot that is a quarter-mile away from where you just dropped everyone off. You run from the parking lot to the windsurfer rack and while doing so realize that the sand is hotter than the asphalt and you burn your feet as you painfully sprint the quarter-mile.

You unlock your windsurfer from the rack and carry it to the water, a trip that is about a hundred yards, and drop it there. Your kids are playing with their friends. You run back up to the rack and grab your mast, sail, and boom. You assemble the sail, a fifteen-minute process. A strong wind kicks up and suddenly ten windsurfers launch from the shore outward. You stay behind. Your kids are anxious to get into the water. You tell the kids that they can go swimming right in front of where your board is sitting on the sailing beach. "Let's go," you say. Everyone jumps in and you are all having a great time.

Three minutes into it, a woman drives over to you in a

four-wheel, bright-green-colored John Deere all-terrain vehicle. You assume that she is the beach manager, riding on her official beach vehicle. From the comfort of her leather padded seat she yells, "No swimming on the sailing beach." "Oh, it's OK," you tell her. "I am their dad, and these are our friends. I am here with my windsurfer and the kids just wanted to cool off. We"—you look over to your wife and friends—"will take full responsibility. We have done this before." To which she responds, "No swimming on the sailing beach!" even more loudly than before. "Come on, Dad," your son says, fearing that you will get put in jail if you do not acquiesce. Your friends look at you nervously. "We can't swim here, Daddy," your four-year-old daughter says.

You get out of the water and talk privately to the beach Nazi. Being a corporate executive, you have experience convincing people to do a lot of things and you believe that after a brief conversation with her she will understand your predicament and look the other way. On the walk over to the strict-looking woman sitting in the four-wheeler you think how impressed your family and friends will be when you show them how persuasive you can be. She tells you that this is the sailing beach and not the swimming beach. "No swimming allowed here," she concludes, then twists her throttle and is off to bust another lawbreaker who she notices toward the south end of the beach.

You announce to your wife, your kids, your friends' kids, and your friends that you have another idea. As you announce this, you look out and the wind is still blowing strongly and coming from the south, so there are no waves. These ideal conditions, of high winds originating from the south and flat water, are a rare combination on this sailing beach and you want to take full advantage of them, but first you must take care of your disappointed kids, wife, friends' kids, and your friends.

"This is my idea," you say. "Let's take three steps over this way"—you point to the private beach. "We will take the board and the kids can dive off it." Everyone is excited. "He is so creative," you think your friends are commenting to themselves about you, even though that is the furthest thing from their minds now.

The kids are psyched. You get the board and push it out into the water, toward the private beach. "It's OK here," you tell your kids. Your kids and your friends' kids pile on the board and they are having the time of their lives. They paddle around with the board and where it is deep they jump off. They all stand on it and try to balance it. For them, this is the best day of the summer so far. You think that your friends think that you are great for turning their kids on to this new activity. Everyone is having great fun. Your vision is realized.

Not so fast, cowboy. From the eight-figure house that is adjacent to the sailing beach but on the private beach, a woman emerges. You notice her walking toward you. She looks mean and she looks like she is on a mission. She senses that you are the person to talk to in this situation. This woman is one of your neighbors, a woman whom you have not yet seen at a party, school function, or anywhere else around town. She storms over to you and points to a sign, which you have noticed and ignored, which says,

PRIVATE BEACH
NO TRESPASSING

She tells you that you are on *her* property, that this is a private beach, and that the beach on the other side of the fence is the public sailing beach. "Could you move over there," she says, not asks. Beautiful, you think, another opportunity to exercise your skills of persuasion. You describe your situation to her and tell her the long story of how you told your friends to come here, how the kids are finally having fun, and how this will be the last time that you encroach on her privacy. "Just this once," you plead. "It is a very hot day and we are just trying to do something fun with the kids." She does not care about any of it. She wants you off *her* property. If she lets you on, she says, she must let everyone on. At that moment, you vow to yourself that if you are ever fortunate enough to own a home that is so terrifically located you will always provide public access to people who are enjoying and respecting it.

Always looking for a positive spin, you turn to your family and friends and announce, "Hey, who wants to go over to the swimming beach?" Your idea is met with less than enthusiastic expressions from everyone until you and the guys peel off alone to start hauling up all the beach gear. "Maybe Blake's Spanish teacher, Ms. What's-Her-Name"—who they have all heard about—"is over there."

The next week, you go to the swimming beach and take a walk with your family along the beach. Losing track of where you are, you look up to notice that you are already at the private beach. There is one curious thing, however. The sign that last week read

PRIVATE BEACH
NO TRESPASSING

has been painted black and is spray-painted with the words

NUDE BEACH

Learn How to Kite Surf

Your friend Stephen windsurfs. You also windsurf, but you have never done this activity with him. You are talking to him one day about a new neighbor in your suburb, the twenty-one-year-old son-in-law of a man who owns a national business you will refer to as an oil-changing and lubricating company. This son-in-law is lucky in that he got the right woman, the lubricating king's daughter, pregnant.

Since they haven't a place to call home, Dad buys the couple, immediately after their rapidly arranged wedding, a $4-million fixer-upper that is on the water. You hear that Dad gave this fortunate couple, with their well-lubricated cars, a matching grant to fix the place up, you know, to make it tolerable.

The home is right on the lake, and being on the lake inspires water activities. Your friend talks to this oil-and-lubrication beneficiary about windsurfing, something that the lubrication kid wants to try. The kid tries out this sport, which is a lot like learning how to ride a bike. You have to understand how to balance, and once you do that it becomes second nature. Before you do, though, it is just hard work. On that day of learning how to windsurf, the lubrication kid kind of gets it and likes it.

Your quick-witted and funny friend has an idea. He has always wanted to go kite-surfing but has never had the opportunity. The equipment is expensive and it is specialized. Knowing that you all like to believe that you are terrific athletes, he tells the lubrication kid, "Shit, you really got the hang of this today. You picked up windsurfing faster than anyone I know. How did you like it?" "I love it, man" is the lubrication kid's response. "If you like windsurfing, you should try kite-surfing. Have you seen that before?" "What's that?" the lubrication kid inquires. "Well, you have this surfboard with straps. Separate from that, there is a massive kite made out of high-tech Kevlar. It is ribbed with titanium battens. The kite is attached to two handgrips by four one-hundred-foot-long guy wires. You fly the kite, then strap on the board and off you go."

You have seen this equipment in the windsurfing store, and because it is so specialized and so few people kite surf, the equipment is fabricated in very small quantities. Because this equipment is made in such small quantities, it is hugely expensive. A setup costs more than $7,500.

Your friend tells his new friend, the oil-and-lubrication kid, that if he bought a kite-surfer your friend would teach him how to use it. "With your ability, you would be all over this lake after a day," your friend says encouragingly, thinking of his own interests as he makes this comment.

The next weekend at the beach—well, you should say that everyday is a "weekend" for this lubrication kid—he shows up fully equipped with his brand-new kite-surfer. With his unique equipment, which most Midwesterners have never seen before, the lubrication kid attracts a lot of attention. He attempts to answer the many questions that are asked of him about his new piece of equipment, but he really has no idea what the correct answers are. He has not figured out that he can just say anything and people will believe him. The only thing missing is his instructor and mentor.

Walking up the beach comes your friend Stephen. "Woo, what do you have there?" he asks. "I picked up a kite-surfer," the lubrication kid says, not being encumbered by the burden of shopping for such an item on the weekend when he has weekday hours available for such an important task.

The oil-and-lubrication kid then asks, "So how do you use this thing? Show me how it works." Your friend turns to the lubrication kid/kite-surfer and admits, "I have no idea. I have never tried a kite-surfer in my entire life, but let's figure it out."

That day your clever friend takes his first ride on a kite-surfer, something he has been wanting to do without spending the money to buy one since he first saw an article on the sport in *Windsurfer* magazine.

Go to Your Block Party

Block parties are a pretty big deal in your suburb. Most of the people you know live on streets that have block parties. And most of them, yourself included, have this tendency to tell people who live on other blocks how great their block party is. What you mean, but are too polite to say, is that your block party is probably better than theirs, which really means that your neighbors are more fun and more interesting than theirs, meaning that the quality of your life is better than the quality of theirs. Block-party tangibles comprise things like who has their block party catered and by whom, who brings in the most elaborate games—like jump houses, petting zoos, and pony rides—and who has the most people attend. These events are discussed among friends who live on different streets and compete with one another in an unspoken competition.

You think that there can be no better block party than yours, because you think that you have the best neighbors in your suburb. However, in talking with your non-neighbor friends, you have difficulty block-party competing, because you cannot describe a set of tangibles at your block party that will compare to theirs. The boccie and the Ping-Pong that you played at your block party last year, while fun, will pale in comparison with the white-tablecloth, catered, and tented affair that they had, with the pony rides on the side. So you do not bring up this topic, and you know that when someone else does it will be their opportunity to tell you about how over-the-top their block is. It is in the middle of these conversations that you usually have to excuse yourself to go to the bathroom or get another drink.

But all this changes for you this year. This year, one of your neighbors, who is a drummer for Smashing Pumpkins, will perform at your block party with a group of his musician friends that you will refer to as Smashing Pumpkins, even though they technically aren't, because it sounds so much better when you discuss the topic with your neighbors. This is interesting for a few reasons. In this suburb of businesspeople, doctors, lawyers, and premature retirees, Matt is the only guy who has green hair and an eyebrow ring and who wears biker boots and tight leather pants. He is an artist, and artists are a rare breed in your suburb. What is also interesting is that Matt is the next-door neighbor of another artist, a guy who writes movies like *Inspector Gadget*, *George of the Jungle*, *The Burbs*, and others that you are not aware of. It's funny that the only two professional artists you know, who live in your suburb, live right next door to each other, and they tell you that this was not a planned event.

The block-party committee—yes, there is a committee, because very little is spontaneous in your suburb and most things are planned and organized by planning committees—has asked Matt if he would play music this year. He said yes, and this is big stuff because Smashing Pumpkins is the hottest rock band in the world. Word of this has spread fast among your neighbors. You have plenty of lead time on this one to initiate many conversations with your non-block friends. You are confident that, no matter what caterers anyone hires, how many ponies they bring in, how large the tent is, or whatever the theme of the jump house may be, you will have something cooler going on at your block party this year. You are confident that you will win any block-party competitive discussion this year.

On this particular July Saturday, late in the afternoon, your block will have its annual summer block party. You get barricades from your suburb's department of public works in the morning. Your first task is to barricade the street from any cars. The kids will emerge and begin riding their bikes and start playing volleyball, boccie, Ping-Pong, Frisbee, and all the other games that come out for this big event. You help with the games, the tables, and anything that you can. Matt is out, too, and he is setting up the speakers, the amplifiers, and the instruments. There are wires and wires, going from his house to the sidewalk in front of his house. It takes a couple of hours to set up this music equipment. Why, you think, as he is setting up this equipment, does it always take bands so long to get set up? Can't anyone figure out a faster way to do it?

Anyway, there it is, right on the sidewalk, a complete setup for the band, and not just any band but Smashing Pumpkins, one of the few bands that have emerged in the past thirty years that you have heard of. You are very appreciative of your good friend Matt for doing this. Because, when you think about it, what will be a block party for everyone else will be an evening of work for Matt; Matt performing at your block party would be the equivalent of you being invited to next year's block party to entertain your neighbors by, say, describing a clever and complicated deal structure that you have created to buy a building, at a fair price, from a seller who was not contemplating a sale.

Anticipation builds all day. Usually, when the block party starts at 3 P.M., people start emerging from their houses at 3:30 or so. This year is different. It is 2:30 and the crowd is already bigger than it was last year. The talk at this event is almost all about Matt and his famous band. Matt is there and you hang out with him. You thank him for working when you will be partying and you try not to embarrass yourself by revealing to him how little you know about Smashing Pumpkins. You try to keep the conversation with Matt general, really general, so that it does not become obvious how ignorant you are about what it is that he does. Then you think that he probably knows less about what you do than you know about what he does, and that maybe it's not such a big deal after all. He may, in fact, be taking the same approach with you, now that you think of it.

The party is in full swing now and you are psyched. The games are rolling and the egg toss has just concluded. The food is coming out and it is nearing 8 P.M., the hour when Matt and his famous band will begin playing.

However, the thing that you have observed about bands is that they never start playing when they say they will. Eight P.M. in your world means 8 P.M. At about 8:35 P.M. or so, four guys emerge with Matt out of Matt's house, with their work clothes on. They all wear mostly tight black clothes and seem overdressed for this warm July evening. One, not deterred by the ninety-degree evening with 90 percent humidity, wears a checkered flannel shirt. No wholesale suits in this crowd.

They approach their instruments and you can feel the excitement build among your neighbors and all the other people you do not recognize as your neighbors. Just as they start playing their first number, "Today," probably the only song that you will recognize on this night, one of your son's friends comes running over to you. "Blake and Ryan just ran into each other on their bicycles," your kid's friend says. "I think that Blake is hurt," he concludes. You run over to where the kids have gathered and, sure enough, your kid, with his bike on the ground and his front wheel twisted, is there, along with his friend Ryan and Ryan's damaged bike.

Your kid has really hurt his arm and his knee is scraped up

badly. He needs to go home to get an ice pack on his arm and take care of his cut. And someone needs to take him. You look around for a volunteer and realize that you are the man for this job. Going for the quick turnaround, you carry him home, quickly clean the cut, and put ice on his arm. He starts to feel a little better, but he does not want to go back to the block party. In your effort to persuade your son to return to the party, you tell him that this world-famous band is playing. "Smashing Pumpkins," you tell him. "Haven't you heard of them?" It takes you fifteen minutes, but you convince him to go back.

You start heading over and you see your wife coming toward you with your daughter. "It is an hour past Bianca's bedtime and she is a wreck," your wife announces to you. Hearing this makes your son want to go back inside, because he does not want his sister getting any special mom-attention that he is not. Your wife asks you to come along to help put the kids to bed. The music gets fainter as you get closer to your house.

You all go home and you volunteer to put your son to bed. You figure it will take you ten, maybe fifteen minutes max, then you are back on the street jamming with the Pumpkins. You go through your evening ritual: read, lights out, story, and Catholic prayer. He wants you to lie down with him, because the music is keeping him up. You do, and you fall asleep.

You wake up after receiving one of his elbows in your face as he turns in his sleep and you notice it is 2:13 A.M. You slip into your bed, and as you are doing so you wake up your wife. You go to sleep; she cannot. You wake up the next morning and call your neighbors to hear how Matt and his famous band were. They cannot stop raving. "Wasn't that the most unbelievable night?" your friend says, not aware that you left one minute into the first set. "It sure was," you respond.

One evening, a week later, you are at a non-block friend's house for a dinner party. You are asked about your block party, because he and his other guests are curious about this famous rocker playing with his band at your block party. This will be a question you will be asked frequently over the next year.

You tell them that it was one incredible night that you will never forget.

Learn About the High School Your Kids Will Attend

Because your social circle has been formed mostly around your elementary-school-aged kids' friends' parents, you know only a very few people who have kids in your local high school, and those people are ones who also have kids your kids' ages. Your wife is a little intimidated by the high school. It is big, with something like two thousand kids per graduating class. You have heard that it is intense. That the options and opportunities there are endless. You have heard that selecting classes is like selecting classes at a really good college. There are hundreds of clubs and the sports teams attract the best of the best. The culture, as you understand it, is that doing well is good (and all the kids want to do well), unlike where you went to high school, where if you wanted to do well you would conceal it.

This school is the reason that you and all your neighbors paid three times more for your homes than you would have if they were located in some other suburb, and also the reason that your taxes are the highest in the country and keep getting higher. You realize that the gene pool that this school draws from is one that would make Charles Darwin proud.

While there is something intimidating about this high school, ultimately you see mainly options and opportunities. And your job is to prepare your kids for this high school by exposing them to enough so that they begin to figure out what they want to do by the time they enter high school; you try to help them identify things at which they excel, because it is your sense that everyone excels at something at this high school.

You are at your block party and you meet a new neighbor. He has a son, whom you also meet for the first time at this block party, and who is in this high school that your kids will attend. He has just completed his sophomore year, and you talk to him and his dad to get some insight into the experience that you will have when your kids get to high school.

The sophomore tells you of the architecture classes that he is taking and the buildings that he has designed using a computer-aided design (CAD) program. He tells you that he has made a movie in one of his after-school clubs and that he is playing baseball, not on the regular team but on an intramural team, which he describes as fun. You presume that he is athletic and that in any other high school he might have been a starting shortstop, but at this high school, where the grooming for baseball begins with a second-grade Little League draft, he has no chance. He tells you that he has created his own website and that if you want to see his movie, his building, or some other cool stuff you can log on to www.bstauter.com. You do not have a website and you have not designed a building. You have not made a movie. You realize that this sophomore has outstripped you and you have two and a half decades on him. He has won this competition that only you know the two of you are having.

He talks about his course load and tells you that he does homework until at least eleven o'clock each evening. He tells you that all of his friends do, too.

Finally, you ask him about grading and how well, in general, other kids do. He says casually that everyone does well. He tells you that there are a lot of smart people and everyone tries very hard. "You have to," he says, "just to keep up." Then he tells you a story that you will repeat often to your other friends, who, like you, do not get much exposure to the high-school scene. He tells you that his cumulative average in his sophomore year was 97.5 out of 100. When you were in high school, that would mean that if you were given 100 things to know you knew 97.5 of them. That would be impressive and it would be something that you would hide from your friends, because you would not want them to get the impression that you were trying too hard.

This sophomore's dad, who is listening to this discussion with interest, then tells you that his son is in the seventy-fourth percentile with his 97.5 grade point average. To you, this means that his son, with his 97.5 grade point average, has a better average than only 74 percent of his two thousand fellow sophomores. It also means that 26 percent, or 520 of them, have a better average then he does, better than 97.5. You are astounded upon hearing this, and your expression shows it. How could you have that kind of grade point average and be in the seventy-fourth percentile? you think. In the high school you attended that GPA would have landed someone in the ninety-ninth percentile.

The kid's dad goes on to explain that there is a weighting system for the level of difficulty of each class; because there are many opportunities for taking college courses and other accelerated classes, many of your neighbor's kid's fellow students have ended up with grade point averages that *exceed* 100. "It is very competitive," he says. You wonder where these kids get their competitive spirit.

First thing tomorrow morning, you reach up to your bookshelf for one of your old ninth-grade algebra textbooks and begin reviewing with your second-grade son how to solve for x.

Have Friends Over for Dinner

Your wife has the idea to have an outdoor dinner party, and you think it is a terrific idea. You run around with the kids in the morning and you hope that the biggest job you will have that day is to take the kids out of the house so they do not interfere with your wife's preparations. Your fantasy is shattered when you receive a call on your cell phone. "Where have you been?" your wife asks. "It is two P.M. and there is a lot to do."

You arrive home and kick into gear. You help set the table, you make sure there is enough gas in the grill—because you have not yet invested in an underground gas line that perpetually feeds your grill, like many of your neighbors have—and you go shopping for beer, wine, and ice. This is usually your main job for dinner parties, a job that you sort of enjoy. It is a job that takes you out of the house when your wife is concerned that everything on the list that she prepared on her 1984 Macintosh SE will be checked off.

This evening, your wife has assembled three other couples whom you and she know but who do not know each other, with the exception of Patty's husband, Donald, whom neither of you has previously met. Your friends show up and there are a series of one-on-one and triangular conversations taking place. On a small-group level, things are jelling. You have gotten a few conversations going and are confident that you can leave your guests unattended for a little bit while you focus on grilling the salmon. Your guests all seem to be getting along and there is commonality among them. It is mostly men talking to men and women talking to women.

There are discussions about where people grew up, an important ritual at a first meeting, to establish who among you comes from the most money. And there is talk about vacations, to see who will be going to the most exotic place this summer. There is also talk about what activities your kids participate in, to determine who has the most gifted kids, and which dads coach the most sports, to determine who is the most engaged dad among this new group of friends. Finally, there are discussions about where everyone lives, to determine who is at the top of this food chain. The only topic that usually surfaces during these introductory neighborhood gatherings that has not yet surfaced is that of block parties. You make a mental note not to be presumptuous in bringing up this topic, with which you know you will win, but you will keep that topic in your back pocket, just in case.

Niceties aside, and pecking orders established, the salmon is done and you are all ready to sit at the table. Everyone sits down and you bring over the food. Food is passed around and it appears that there are eight full plates, eight full glasses of wine, and eight full glasses of water. The kids are sitting at the kids' table.

To kick off the first conversation that this newly formed group will engage in, Donald, Patty's husband, whom all of the guests, including you and your wife, are meeting for the first time, commands the attention of everyone at the entire table. You guess that he has an icebreaker to get the conversation rolling, perhaps one he has tried before with success. As he makes eye contact with everyone around the table, he says he has a question to ask of everyone. "Let me ask you all a question, one that I am very curious about," he says. "Are women as turned on by the thought of two guys being together sexually as guys are at the thought of two women together sexually?" Apparently, Donald is embracing diversity and he wants to show you all how he is living up to your suburban motto.

Your new acquaintance has certainly grabbed your attention and the attention of all of your guests, who you assume are now wondering to themselves, How do the Falangas know this guy? Your wife, the only one bold enough to address this icebreaker, responds, "Absolutely not." She admits to all that the thought of two guys together sexually does absolutely nothing for her, and you are relieved with her response to what you had assumed was a rhetorical question. The other women concur.

Donald now looks at the guys with an expression that indicates he would like the male perspective on this important-to-him topic. Your male guests, like you, realize that this is a dangerous question to address in such a crowd, a question with no right answer. You feel that it is incumbent on you to set the tone and to respond to this off-the-wall question, a question to which there is no good answer in this crowd of newly formed acquaintances, and a question the motivation of which you are not sure of.

You look at your guests and transition the conversation by saying, "What are you all doing for your block parties this summer?"

Attend the Fortieth Birthday of Your Neighbor

You are invited to a neighbor's fortieth-birthday party. You are an acquaintance of this neighbor but you have not socialized with the couple, except at an occasional holiday party. They seem like very nice people.

Just about every party that you go to in your suburb is a party where people stand, drink, eat, and move around, or it's a dinner party where you talk mostly to the people at your table. Because your suburb is relatively small, you usually know most people at each party you go to. You arrive at this party, a summer, backyard party. You enter the backyard, and because you are showing up fashionably late a crowd has assembled. You look around and are surprised that you do not recognize one single person at this party of, say, 120 people. However, everyone else but you seems to know one another. In the five years that you have lived in your suburb, this has never, ever happened. You conclude that no one attending this party is from your suburb. Where they are from? You have no idea.

You go to grab a beer so that you can look purposeful at this party where you do not know anyone but your wife, and you soon realize that there is none. You find out that this is an alcohol-free fortieth-birthday party, your second indication within two minutes that this party will be different from all the others you have attended. You substitute an apple juice for the beer, because there is no purple grape juice, either; apple juice is such a great help to you in opening up to a yard full of strangers.

The guests are then asked to take a seat, any seat. There are about twelve or fifteen tables placed in the backyard, each having a capacity of ten people. You and your wife look around to see which group of strangers looks most inviting. You are equally unacquainted with everyone there, so you conclude that one table is like another. You choose the first two empty seats that you see at a table that is close to the back of the house.

You think that you are sitting down to eat dinner, but you are wrong. Larry, the guest of honor, walks up to a microphone that you have not noticed until now and invites his guests to come up and say "what they feel." What appears to you to be an uncomfortable silence descends over the crowd and you are nervous for Larry that on his fortieth birthday nobody will come up to the mike and say anything, because you know that you will not and you assume that most people are like you. About this, however, you are wrong.

As soon as Larry is seated, a small line of people who have something to "share with you" about Larry begins to form. They say, "I have something that I would like to share with you about Larry." You have heard people use the word "share" before in this context and it usually means that it will be serious, heartfelt, maybe even spiritual, and not funny.

The first woman, who introduces herself as Addie, describes how she met Larry at a self-help group that was first assembled ten years ago and still meets weekly. She is brought to tears as she describes how loving and caring Larry is, two adjectives that do not come to mind when you think of Larry and two adjectives that you would be surprised to hear from Larry's wife and daughter if they were to go up to the mike to speak, which they do not, or from his ninth-grade son, if he were home from his East Coast military boarding school, which he is not. She goes on to say how Larry was the glue that kept the group together, and that because of Larry they are all better off for it. "Larry is an amazing man," she says. You look at your wife, who, like you, cannot believe what she is hearing at this fortieth birthday. You look around to the other guests who are seated at your table and you are compelled to look at someone and say, "Can you believe this shit?" But as you prepare to do so you see some of your table-mates drying their tears with their napkins and two others proceeding to line up behind the microphone to "share" their sentiments about Larry now that Addie has broken the ice. At that moment, you decide against asking anyone your question.

You and your wife do not talk. There is no need to. You know that this is one of those occasions where she is thinking the same exact thing that you are, which is, How do we get the hell out of here? In the meantime, you hear about Larry's "men's group," which spent a week in Oregon. Each member of this particular men's group got up to tell the story of how whining everything they said for an entire week while they were in Oregon made them into better men than they were before. They hugged each other a lot. You are getting a little nervous about the line forming behind the microphone, because to you the stories are getting progressively stranger. You have already learned more about your neighbor than you care to know.

Next, a group of white suburban men (from some distant suburb, you are sure) approaches the microphone and starts playing conga drums. This would be OK, except the conga group has the rhythm of, well, white suburban men. They are members of another men's group that Larry belongs to, a white man's tribal group of some sort. Larry and his tribal men's group start dancing, without any semblance of rhythm, to the beat of the equally rhythmless conga drums. One thing that you are certain of is that, if nothing else, all of Larry's participation in men's groups has given him the self-confidence to be himself in front of a crowd. Before long, most of the 120 guests join Larry and his men's group on the dance floor, each with his or her own interpretation of tribal dancing.

You and your wife take this as your cue to "get home for the babysitter, who has to go home early tonight," if anyone asks. First, your wife goes unnoticed into the back of the house, then a minute later you follow suit and meet her on Larry's front porch.

It is not too late to catch a movie, your wife says. It is the second time that day that you both agree.

Take a Trip to a Foreign Country

You are of Italian descent and you have twenty-five Italian relatives who live in Italy. One is a cousin who your parents and your aunt and uncle have told you looks, talks, and gestures like you. You talk to your wife about going to Italy and she is excited. Because she is a planner, she goes to the library and gets every book about Italy, and each night when you come home she tells you of all the marvelous things that there are to see and do there.

You will go to Milan, Florence, Rome, and Venice. You will go spend a day with your relatives near Sorrento. You will travel along the Amalfi coast and you will go to small towns like Positano and Siena in the Tuscany region. She knows the best things to do and see in each place because she has done her homework. This will be a great trip.

You feel connected to Italy in some ways. Your grandfather immigrated to the United States from Italy in 1920. He arrived in America through Ellis Island, where he is now honored with a plaque. That was a time that a lot of people moved from Italy to the States, because it was no fun in Europe after World War I.

When your grandfather was alive, you always had difficulty understanding him because of his strong accent. He worked hard and said little. When he did say something, everyone listened, because what he said was always worth listening to. He was most comfortable speaking Italian, but he did not around you. He was an American, and Americans speak English. He had an important job in getting his next generation of Americans prepared as best he could.

Your father grew up in a house with your grandfather and grandmother, whose parents also moved to the United States from Italy. Your grandmother spoke Italian, too. Because your grandparents were more comfortable speaking Italian than English, your father spoke Italian as well.

Despite all this Italian language, the only Italian you ever heard growing up was at family gatherings, sitting around a dining room table, when the adults were saying something that they did not want the kids to understand. These conversations were the ones that you listened most closely to, in an effort to understand what the adults felt you shouldn't. At this task you always failed.

After this first trip to Italy, it would become your favorite foreign country and the country that you visit once or sometimes twice a year. You connect with everything in this country, except the language.

On your first trip to this country, where the people respect their elders and where they know how to balance work and hanging out better than anyone in the world, your wife, who has a proclivity for picking up foreign languages, starts to get it. You rely on her to assist you in ordering food in restaurants and asking for directions, the only two things that you find you really have to communicate with the outside world about.

You, on the other hand, after a week of travel, have taken the effort to learn one word, *grazie*, which means "thank you."

You then combine it with the other Italian word that you have brought with you from America, *ciao*, which, during the first two years after you learned this word, you would spell "chow."

In learning this new word, you become the single most polite person in all of Italy. You say *grazie* to everyone, for everything. Your wife will engage in lengthy Italian conversations with people while you stand silent at her side—that is, until the conversation concludes. This is your cue. It is your turn to speak and you say, "*Grazie*." You are a polite American, not like the ugly Americans who do not make the effort to learn the language.

You are amazed at your wife. She has really picked up a lot and she is not shy about putting together new phrases. It is about midway through this trip and you work your way to Sorrento and then to the small town where your family lives, Masse Lubrenze. You arrive at the home of one of your relatives and many come to greet you. They live in a home above the bakery that has been in the family for four generations. Fortunately, there is one woman, whom one of your cousins married, who is Australian and as a result speaks English. Other than that, you, Mr. Grazie, are on your own.

You gather around and all the other relatives, who live minutes away, are summoned. Your twenty-five relatives gather, and Assunta, the Australian, is the person you rely on as your translator. On the other hand, your twenty-five relatives have fallen in love with your wife, who is actually carrying on conversations with them in Italian while they are trying to understand why you are telling them thank you all the time. What impresses you most is that you believe, but are not entirely sure, that your wife is *not* asking them for directions or ordering food from them. She has a house full of twenty-five non–English-speaking Italians captivated. You think that she may be telling them the story of you saying *grazie* all the time. You soon find out differently.

In her conversation, she says something and you see twenty-five startled expressions, then you see a few of your male cousins and uncles—Mario, in particular—laugh, sort of embarrassed, to themselves. Your wife senses that she may have said something that she did not intend to, but, undeterred, she keeps on speaking, in Italian.

Sensing that something is wrong, she looks to Assunta to better understand what has just transpired, to understand why the sudden change in facial expressions. Assunta looks at you and to your wife. The room goes silent and she tells your wife, in English, that she just told your twenty-five Old World relatives, as she thought she was describing the beautiful sights of Florence and the Duomo, that she "loves to suck my husband." This is an expression that has never, you guess, in four generations of Falangas, been uttered in this house. You think this because in your life you have never once heard your mother or father or grandparents ever say a curse, not even "hell" or "damn."

You look around, and your wife, who—if she didn't have anyone's attention before, she does now—looks at them all and starts laughing hysterically. They do, too. And that draws you closer to these Italian relatives than anything else you can do or say. It is a story that you are sure they will repeat often to their friends, and one that you hope will come true.

With your relatives, you see the church that your great-grandfather built and meet other relatives who live in the country in a beautiful old stone house with a small vineyard. These are people who know how to live, you think.

Your entire family is there, because none of the remaining people have moved from this small town in southern Italy except your grandfather and his brother, who moved to Buenos Aires. The rest have stayed put, with one exception, Fabrizzio, who lives in Rome.

After you cement this connection with your family, you are

off to Rome, after telling them *grazie* and *ciao*, to check out the city and visit with Fabrizzio, this cousin of yours who everyone says looks and gestures like you. In Rome, there are many amazing things to see and one of them is the Vatican. To you, this place has meaning. It is where the Pope lives, and when you were a boy growing up it was the origin of the many conservative and rigid rules that governed your life until you were in high school.

You bring your wife to the Vatican, though for her it does not carry the same meaning. However, you cannot help but be taken with the enormousness of the plaza and the tribute that this structure is to the holy. You tour the entire Vatican and you see opulence like you have never seen before in your life. These Italians, when they built the Vatican, built it to show God how much they loved, respected, and regarded Him. They broke the bank on this and did not care about any change orders. To the financiers, architects, and contractors of this marvel, it was their ticket to Heaven; thus there were no limits. Everything was on a grand scale.

Your wife takes this all in and, while usually overly enthusiastic about everything and nothing, she does not react at all throughout your entire Vatican tour. "This is where the Pope lives," you tell her. "That is the window where he makes his Wednesday addresses to the public. Look at the scale of this place, the gold, the marble, the ceiling heights, and all the symbolism and history surrounding you. Can you believe that we are here?" you say.

Your wife, who did not celebrate Christmas while growing up, is unfazed and unmoved. You walk out of the Vatican and into the large oval plaza. As you are walking through the plaza toward the exit, there are a few construction barricades surrounding a yellow John Deere bulldozer, which you know was made in Peoria, Illinois. Apparently, they are doing some routine maintenance at this unroutine structure. Your wife takes note of this common, American-made yellow bulldozer and focuses on the seat. Her eyes widen and her attention is drawn. You know this expression and can tell that she has seen something that excites her. Then she turns to you and says, "Look at the seat on that bulldozer! Could you believe that? It is the most beautiful leather bulldozer seat that I have ever seen! I have never seen anything like that before in my life!" Her reaction to this bulldozer seat reminds you of her reaction to the draperies she noticed years earlier when you toured the White House.

So there you have it: you now know that everyone sees God in different things and in different ways. The big take-away for your wife at the Vatican was seeing the leather seat on the bulldozer, something that you never knew she cared about. God works in mysterious ways, you think.

You arrive back in America, where you can be more than polite. As you reflect on your trip, your wife tells your friends what wonderful bulldozer seats they have in Italy. You imagine your uncles, Mario and Sergio, talking among themselves, recapping the trip. You think they say, in Italian, "Mark is so polite, and how lucky is he, having such a beautiful wife who loves to suck him."

YOUR
SUBURBAN
FALL

Coach Football

Your second-grade kid wants to play flag football and you think that is great. You volunteer to coach his team, because you enjoy coaching more than you enjoy spectating. You think that it is a great way to spend time with your kid and to get to know his friends. You don't think that you really knew how to play football when you were in second grade. Your memories of playing this sport start in fourth grade, maybe fifth, and you mostly played in the street outside of your suburban Long Island home. When you played, you had plays like "you do a banana," which was running out, in a curved fashion, for a pass. You did "buttonhooks," which meant running out quickly then turning around to catch the ball just as you turned around. You did "down and outs" and "down and ins." You went for the long bomb. Those were your passing patterns. Sometimes you just "went short" for the third completion, which would give you a first down. You had to do all these plays by the count of five Mississippi. Things have changed.

You show up for your flag-football coaches' orientation and are given a playbook as you walk into the classroom. It is labeled "Play Book," because it actually is a book containing the many offensive and defensive plays that your team will run this season.

The league vice president, as you want to call him, tells you that he is the author of "Play Book." He informs you that *any* offensive or defensive plays that your teams will run this season will come from the "Play Book" that is sitting before you right now, the one that you are trying to, but can't really, figure out. You think that it is a good idea for you to understand it first, before getting your second-grade team to embrace it, and you can tell already that you are going to invest more time in your football-coaching effort this season than you were anticipating.

"Play Book" is perfect-bound and it has pages and pages of plays. It is, you would estimate, a little over half an inch thick. There are Xs and Os delineating offensive and defensive players, and straight and curved lines with arrows showing running patterns for each of the Xs and Os. You flip through "Play Book" and you do not see buttonhooks, bananas, down and outs, down and ins, long bombs, or going short. In fact, there is nothing that is really familiar to you at all in "Play Book." You realize that you will not be handing down the traditions of your football youth to your kid and his teammates during this football season.

To further complicate things, each offensive and defensive play that your team will be deploying this football season has a fancy, impossible-to-remember name that perhaps made sense to the league vice president when he was busy during the off-season crafting this book, but will be meaningless to you and your team. There is not even anything close to the self-explanatory names that you gave your plays as a youth. Here is what some of the plays are called:

Center Curl-back Short-right End Long Left End Medium
Center Medium Left End Around Short-back Right Long
QB Handoff to Back and QB Right Short-right End Short
    Turnout Center Medium-left End Long

You know that you are going to have a terrific time this football season explaining these plays to your second-grade team. There is a section in "Play Book" called "Defensive Plays." When you were a kid and you played defense, you simply tried to match up with a kid on the other team who was about as athletic as you. It went something like this: "I got Ray," meaning that for the entire game you would go anywhere and everywhere Ray would go, or that was the idea, anyway. While it didn't always work out like that, if nothing else you understood what you were supposed to do.

There is no such advice in "Play Book." The defensive plays in your book are mostly what you would call zone defense, the idea being that, rather than covering one kid wherever that kid would go, you cover a territory, say, five yards by five yards, or twenty-five square yards. With the defensive plays outlined in "Play Book," labeled *Two-Three, Two-Two-One*, and names like that, each team member's job is to deal with anything that happens within his territory. You regard zone defense as a bit more of an abstract concept than man-to-man, and you assume that your second-grade players will too.

You and all the other coaches are told again during this orientation meeting that all the plays you run this season must be from "Play Book." You ask jokingly if you can slip in a buttonhook or a banana every once in a while and the league vice president does not laugh. He asks if there are any other questions. There are none.

Then the league vice president hands out a separate book called "Rule Book," which is about half an inch thick. You believe that the league vice president is the author of the "Rule Book" as well, although in your coaches' orientation he doesn't claim authorship, like he did for "Play Book." One thing for sure is that the league vice president has been very busy during the off-season.

What's interesting about "Rule Book" is that the rules are very different from the way that football is really played and also different from the rules that your second-grade boys will be familiar with. As coach, it will be your job to make sure that, in addition to your team gaining a full understanding of the plays outlined in "Play Book," you must also make sure they understand the rules outlined in "Rule Book."

Some of the rules in "Rule Book" are as follows:

The offensive team takes possession of the ball at its 5-yard line and has three (3) plays to cross midfield. Once a team crosses midfield, it has three (3) plays to score a touchdown. If the offensive fails to score, the ball changes possession and the new offensive team takes over on its 5-yard line.

Interceptions change the possession of the ball at the point of interception. Interceptions are the only changes of possession that do not start on the 5-yard line.

Each time the ball is spotted a team has 30 seconds to snap the ball. Teams will receive one warning before a delay-of-game penalty is enforced.

This last rule referenced is particularly interesting to you because what you interpret it to mean is that in each huddle you will have a maximum of thirty seconds to explain to your second-grade team how to, say, run the *Center Medium Left End Around Short-back Right Long* play or the *QB Handoff to Back and QB Right Short-right End Short Turnout Center Medium-left End Long*. No sweat, plenty of time.

You walk out of your orientation meeting with documents that are more than one inch thick, realizing that you know much less about football than you thought you did an hour before. You realize that your key competitive challenge this season will be between you and "Play Book" and "Rule Book."

Go on a Treasure Hunt

You come home from work one day and squeeze your German luxury car into the ultra-narrow space that your wife allocated for it in your garage because she wanted to make sure that she had plenty of room for herself and your five-year-old, thirty-five-pound daughter to disembark from the SUV and walk to the service door. You squeeze out of your car trying not to ding any panel on either of these overpriced vehicles, because you know that removing a ding from either of these two cars will cost at least one zero more than removing dings from other regular cars.

You then sashay between the two cars, because there is not enough room to walk straight on, and you are thin. You maneuver around the back of the SUV and then breathe easy along the homestretch, where there is enough room for you, your entire family, and your neighbor's kids, if they were so inclined, to walk six abreast.

As you approach the windowed service door to exit the garage, you observe an item in your backyard that you have never before noticed. It is huge, almost flat—except for the two warped surfaces—faded green, with a rusted metal base. The wood on top and along the edges is delaminated and appears to have swelled with moisture. It's a Ping-Pong table. It is warped, it is coming apart, it is chipped, and it is in *your* backyard. You like Ping-Pong, and in fact you played Ping-Pong frequently with your uncle when you were a kid. You think that perhaps you can fit in a few games with your kids before this monster in your backyard disappears and goes back to wherever it belongs.

As you walk past the table, you wonder how it got there and who may have brought it there. You wonder why it did not end up in someone else's yard. Why my yard? you ask yourself. You can't think of any scenario that makes sense.

As you go inside, your son comes running up to you, and, more excited than you have seen him about many things in his life, he says, "Dad, Dad, did you see the Ping-Pong table in the backyard? We got it for free." "For free?" you ask, in mock amazement, really thinking, How much did someone pay my son for him to store this piece of shit in our yard, and, Whatever they paid him, it is not enough.

He responds, "Yeah, we found it in the alley." "Who found it in the alley?" "Ed, Tom, and I found it." "Who else was with you with when you found it?" you ask, probing to see what adult would be responsible for this atrocity in your backyard. "Mom was with us." "Mom let you bring that home and put it in our yard?" "Yeah, Ed and Tom's moms would not let us put it in their backyards," your son says, answering the question that had previously formed in your mind as to why this Ping-Pong table didn't land in someone else's yard. "Oh? I wonder why not?" you ask jokingly. "Could you believe that someone was throwing away this Ping-Pong table? It must be worth $1,000," he says. You are not sure how to reply to this, knowing that the only appropriate place for this Ping-Pong table is in a landfill in someone else's suburb. "The people let us take it, could you believe that?" he says, sparing you the agony of answering his last question. "We need to get a net, ball, and paddles," he says excitedly. Your wife enters the room and it is clear that she shares your kid's enthusiasm for the table. She has told your son how Daddy can fix up the table with a little paint and glue. You look at her in utter disbelief, knowing that the only appropriate fix for this Ping-Pong table is putting it in a landfill.

You go to the sports store and buy all the equipment you need to get this table fully functioning, a $58 investment. On this trip, you think how you are going to break it to your son that your yard is an *inappropriate* place for this beat-up old Ping-Pong table, and that if it stays there long enough your fear is that it may prompt a falling-out with your neighbors. You conclude that you will wait and have a discussion with your wife to figure out how to get rid of this monstrosity without crushing your kid's enthusiasm.

That night, after the kids are asleep, you bring up the topic of the Ping-Pong table with your wife, who has this idea that it will take you an hour to fix up this table, which is irreparable and lacks portability. She is shocked at your suggestion that this new Ping-Pong table, which has become the centerpiece of your yard, is in bad shape. "I thought you could fix anything," she says.

You understand now that your wife does not see this table as the albatross that you do, which is surprising to you, given how an out-of-place pair of shoes (yours) in the entryway area of your home annoys her so much that she is compelled to move them to where they cannot be found. You understand that you will not be co-strategizing the removal of this table with your wife.

Immediately after your discussion, she calls her friend, the stay-at-home-mom chair expert, and two others, and gets their opinions about keeping the Ping-Pong table or not. None of them have seen the table, yet they all have backed your wife in her effort to keep the table in your yard. Better in your yard than theirs, you think that they are thinking. Your wife, now armed with the backing of her friends, has locked in on her position to keep this piece of junk in your yard. You know now that there is no way that you will win this argument with reason and logic.

You remember that your kids have been talking about a yard sale and you develop a strategy for eradicating this pile of garbage from your yard.

Have a Lawn Sale

After looking out on that Ping-Pong table in your yard for two weeks now, and thinking about how that falling-apart thing may negatively impact your relationships with your neighbors, you announce to your family that you have an idea. At the dinner table one night you say, "Let's have a yard sale." This is one of the rare instances in the history of your family where, for different reasons, everyone responds positively to your idea. Your wife is a great cleaner and organizer, and this is something that, although unspoken between you and her, will be her responsibility to take on. She is enthusiastic. Her idea is that you create a neighborhood lawn sale that involves, say, six or eight families. The bigger the better, is your reaction. She wants to get rid of clutter, like the time when she sold the trumpet that you grew up with, for $15, because it was cluttering the storage closet.

Your sole motivation for introducing this concept to your family is to get rid of the Ping-Pong table, and you have three obstacles to overcome. The first is convincing your son that he would somehow be better off without the table that he found and wheeled into your yard that Wednesday afternoon two weeks ago with your wife supervising. The second is convincing your wife of the same, which will probably be your biggest challenge. Her support of this rusted, delaminated, warped, and faded forty-five-square-foot-consuming piece of shit baffles you and is inconsistent with everything you know about her. She is usually very fastidious about things of this nature, or you assume that she is, because you know that every time you put your keys on the newly decorated entryway table it bothers her so much that she is compelled to move your keys to a place where you can never find them and then gets angry at you when you ask her where she has put them. The third obstacle to overcome is to provide a way to get rid of it.

It appears that you have addressed the third obstacle by coming up with the idea for the yard sale. You then figure that if you can get your kid to embrace the idea of selling the Ping-Pong table then your wife will go along. You talk it over privately with your son. You let him know how much you love Ping-Pong, which you do, and you let him know how much you love to play Ping-Pong with him, which you do. You call his attention to the rust and delaminating edges, the warped surfaces, and the faded color of the Ping-Pong table, and the amount of space it takes up in your yard.

You explore alternatives with him, like perhaps getting another Ping-Pong table, a new one that is made to be placed outdoors. Not quite convinced that this is the right move, you then tell him that he can sell it for whatever price he would like and keep all the money. A figure of $800 pops into his head (a $200 discount off of what he initially valued the table at) and he thinks that will go a long way to getting the laptop that he has been wanting for a year or so. You talk him down to something more realistic, say $100, knowing that it will probably cost you $100 to get rid of this white elephant. He believes that this is the way to go. He is sure this is the right thing. "Good decision," you say. "Now go convince Mommy." Well, he does, and he is excited.

The ads are in place and signs are posted around the neighborhood. The eight participating families haul all of their now unused toys, clothes, and other stuff over to the Swensens'. Their lawn becomes littered with brightly colored blow-molded plastic trucks, cars, and ironing boards. There are CDs, TVs, slides, plastic swimming pools, all the stuff that was once the mainstay of your kids' existence. You realize that, at eight years old, your son is no longer a child. His toys are real now, his music is grown-up, and his clothes are like yours, only cooler. He wants laptops, skis, and other stuff like that, which you like too.

It is morning and there is optimism when prices are set. The kids are actively involved in setting prices, with the basic formula being bigger equals more expensive. While the lawn sale was advertised to start at 10 A.M., many people show up at 8:30. You sell off whatever you can. Now that you have gotten the Ping-Pong table in this sale, your next objective is to not have to haul anything back to your house. "Sell everything," you tell the kids. "If someone looks at all interested in anything on the lawn, offer them a price and get rid of it." "Everything goes" is your mantra. And it does.

By midday, you have detected little customer interest in the Ping-Pong table. Not that you are really surprised, but for you it was the only reason for initiating this sale. If you do not get rid of it, you will judge the sale a failure. You think that if you begin playing Ping-Pong on the table your customers will see how much fun they could have with it and that they will then buy it. How they will get it home, you are not sure.

Ken, the neighbor across the street, who is not selling anything in the sale, comes out and you challenge him to a game. He has a great time and you let him win. You say, "Ken, this would be a terrific addition to your backyard, don't you think? You are a talented player. Just think how often you could play and how good you would get if the table was in your yard each and every day." He looks at you and says, "There is no way that I would ever put this piece of shit in my yard. Don't even think about it." He says this knowing exactly what you have in mind. He leaves, saying that he has to go down to the office for a few hours.

You arouse interest in the game and everyone wants to play. It is 3:45 and you have another fifteen minutes to sell this dog, when Carol, Ken's wife, steps out of her car and sees the Ping-Pong table. She is excited. She tells you how much her husband, Ken, loves Ping-Pong. Her teenage daughter, who has gotten out of the car with Carol, tells her mother that she loves Ping-Pong too. "Can we get it, Mom?" she asks. You reinforce Carol's impression. "Carol, you know, Ken was here earlier playing Ping-Pong with me, and I have never seen him so happy. He is a great player." You add, "He even beat me. It would be a terrific surprise for him. Your daughter is enthusiastic. It would be a wonderful thing to do for her. She will be going off to college pretty soon. There will be fewer and fewer opportunities to bring the kind of happiness and joy to your teenager than the opportunity that you will have today to buy this Ping-Pong table. I will even deliver and install it." You are laying it on because Carol is the only person all day who has showed any interest in the Ping-Pong table and is probably your last chance, despite the fact that her husband, Ken, told you an hour earlier that there was no way he wanted anything to do with that piece of shit.

You make this last representation because Carol lives just across the street from the Swensens' yard. It is closer to her house than yours. You tell Carol that you will inspect her yard with her. "Let's find the perfect spot for it," you say to Carol.

Her daughter comes as well, and before even going into the backyard you find the spot that was made for this Ping-Pong table, on one side of their house. "Carol," you say, "there is no better location in this entire suburb for this Ping-Pong table than right here. It will be right off of your side door, in an easy-to-get-to location. It will not take up any precious backyard space and will bring happiness into your family like you have never known." You add, "Just think of Ken's expression when he comes home."

Carol laughs, because you think she knows that you just want to get rid of this thing, but she seems to be enjoying your pitch. You announce to Carol that the price has dropped from $100 to $10.

Carol looks at her daughter, who is beaming with encouragement, and says the words you have been hoping to hear: "OK, bring it over." Without hesitating, you enlist the help of your friend to assist you wheel it over. You collect $10 and pass that along to your kid.

So When Did Halloween Become Such a Big Deal?

For the entire month of October, you will obsess about what you will be for Halloween, because you have already been invited to two Halloween parties and it is not yet even October 1. You do not have any idea yet what you will be and you know that you will have to outdo the police uniform that you came up with last year; it was fun to bust your neighbors, showing up to the Kostases' party at 11:30 P.M., telling them that a neighbor complained about the noise and could they please keep it down, otherwise you would have to arrest some people.

Halloween was once a minor, second-tier kids' holiday, but it has somehow snuck up on you and become a big-deal grown-up holiday. It is also different from most other big holidays: for Christmas, the Fourth of July, Easter, Thanksgiving, and New Year's, you just need to show up. Not for Halloween. Not anymore. This is a holiday that each year requires more and more creativity. In your suburb, the bar is set high. People take this holiday seriously; just go by the Franzes' to see how elaborately their house is decorated if you have any doubts about that. There is an annual party with your kids at the

Roushes' that just three years ago was a low-key affair where adults hung out mostly in their kitchen, in their regular clothes, while kids in costumes played around.

This past year, the party moved outside and into a big tent, the kind of tent that is rented from a professional party-rental store that is located somewhere other than the suburb where you live. It is the kind of tent that requires professional assembly, probably union labor working on double time. There is a live band playing as you walk in, and a haunted house in the garage.

Then there is the Lauters' party. This is another annual parent-kid party, and includes a parade around the neighborhood. Parents have to get dressed up for this one too. There is trick-or-treating, which, when you were young, involved you going to your friend's house and a bunch of you going to all the neighbors in the neighborhood. You all dressed up as bums, because it was a costume that you could slap together in fifteen minutes. The days of throwing on a pair of ripped-up pants and a dirty shirt are over.

Each of these parties is a catered affair, with tuxedoed men and women serving from a full bar that was brought in for the occasion, with hors d'oeuvres and main courses served on fine china. There is silver tableware.

You think on this. Could you imagine your parents getting dressed up for Halloween as you do? Could you imagine your father getting dressed up as the cop you were last year? The thought of it is absurd. Yet here you are, you, all your friends, and all your neighbors, getting dressed up for Halloween in ridiculous costumes.

For the entire month of October, the question of what you will be occupies your mind and nothing crops up. You have now been invited to five parties, three adults-only and two family parties, each hosted by friends who have staked out the holiday as theirs. It is the day of your first party and you have not thought of anything clever. You look at the police uniform hanging in your closet from last year and remember how much of a hit you were. You put it on. You go to your first party and you are greeted by Sandy, who comments, "Oh, so you decided to be a policeman again. Very clever." You feel you have let her down. You make a mental note to begin planning your Halloween costume in August of next year.

Get a Haircut

It is the Saturday before Thanksgiving, and you, along with your family, are leaving for a suburb of San Francisco to visit with your sister, her family, and your parents. This will be a family reunion. The relatives whom your family spent each Thanksgiving with when you were growing up in a suburb of New York are also coming. They are coming from Long Island, where you grew up. Your cousin is coming from a town next to Southampton, a town that is always in the *Wall Street Journal*, a town that has become synonymous with the Wall Street market boom of the late nineties. She is coming to this suburb of San Francisco with her family, and her parents, who live a half hour away from her, are coming as well.

You have not seen your immediate family in six months, since your last business trip to San Francisco, and you have not seen your cousin, her family, and your aunt and uncle for a few years.

Since your parents moved from a suburb of New York on Long Island to a suburb of San Francisco, you have little reason to go to Long Island, even though you travel to New York City frequently. You want to make the most favorable impression possible on these favorite relatives of yours, whom you have not seen in a long time, and a good start to that is showing up with the right haircut. You want them to walk away from the experience thinking, Boy, doesn't Mark look good. Still so youthful-looking, thin, and in shape, and what a terrific haircut. This is what you want them to say on the plane trip home and this is what you want them to say when they are folding up the sofa bed and putting the cover back on the hot tub after you leave. You want to look good. You want to look together. You want to look like the corporate executive that you are.

You usually get your haircuts in the big building where you work. You were instrumental in retaining a hair salon run by a guy named Michael. You worked hard to retain Michael because you like having a place in your building where you can go to and get a haircut in twelve minutes. You have worked on this twelve-minute haircut with Sandi, who works for Michael, over several years and she has it down. Sandi is now the only one that you will get a haircut from. She is fast and she knows exactly what haircut you want. A few times when she was not in and you "had" to get your haircut that day, it was a mistake and your friend-boss was the only person man enough to let you know. He was also always nice enough to call your bad haircut to the attention of all of your colleagues.

Well, during the week preceding your Saturday departure for San Francisco you intend to get a haircut from Sandi at Michael's, but by the time you think of it it is Friday. You call down to Michael, who, because you have helped him so much with his business, will always squeeze you in anytime you want. He was the one who set you up with Sandi in the first place. When Michael answers, as he usually does, he will tell you some dirty jokes. Michael likes dirty jokes, and, whatever dirty joke you may have, it is nothing compared with what Michael comes up with. Only his dirty jokes are extracted from his real-life experiences.

Michael has been divorced and he has hired only the most

attractive women to give haircuts and sweep his floors. Michael knows how to give his clientele what they want in a hair salon. He talks about rim jobs and other stuff like that, which you have never heard of and don't quite know what they are but sound like they would feel really good. On that day, Michael reveals to you that Sandi is not in. You know better than to get set up with someone else and you say you will give him a call back next week.

Your hair is shaggy and needs to be cut. You have a dilemma.

The next morning, Saturday, you wake up and you have a 1 P.M. flight that day. You look in the mirror and imagine your relatives, whom you have not seen in such a long time, saying, when you leave them, "Wasn't Mark's hair so shaggy? I thought that he was such a big-shot corporate executive. Why doesn't he get a haircut? I'm sure there is a hair salon in that big building that he tells us he runs." You do not want this to be the dominant impression that your relatives are left with, so that Saturday morning you ask your wife where you should go to get a haircut.

Your wife knows the hair industry. She used to work for a shampoo company, and when she did she tried to convince you that one brand of shampoo was not the same as every other only in a different container. Although she failed to convince you of this myth, she also gets haircuts frequently and you know that she has a lot of discussions with her friends about hair. It is, in fact, usually an introductory conversation with every one of her friends that she sees. "I love your hair. It looks terrific," she always starts out a conversation. "Yours too," her friend would respond. "I love the highlights." "Highlights" is the term that you frequently hear describing what you would call a full blond dye job.

You figure that someone who converses about hair as much as your wife should be able to lay a good barber recommendation on you during this time of need. She does not let you down. She pulls through by responding immediately. "Victor's," she says, brimming with confidence.

You have heard of Victor's because that is where your son goes for his $6 buzz cuts. You call Victor and he tells you, in an Eastern European accent that you could hardly understand, that he has a busy day but that he can squeeze you in right now, if you hurry up and get there. Your wife gives you directions to Victor's, which you realize is located not far away from where you live. You take your son along to keep you company. You like doing anything with either of your kids. You enjoy their company. You rush out of your garage to avoid an alley conversation with David Golob and on the way over you drive by the Franzes' house, which is decked out with Pilgrims, turkeys, and a house-size cornucopia filled with gigantic inflated ears of corn.

You and your son arrive at Victor's. He greets your son like they are old buddies. Victor puts you in his chair and you explain the haircut that you would like from him. You have not had to give these directions to anyone for years, because Sandi knows exactly what to do. It is simple, you tell Victor: short on the sides and back and longer on top. This is the haircut that, twenty years ago, when you last gave this subject any thought, you determined you look best in.

Victor has an interesting arrangement of chairs and mirrors that you have never seen before in any barbershop or hair salon. He has placed a series of round, three-foot-diameter mirrors on the wall, directly opposite the patron's chairs when they are facing forward. He has also placed the same three-foot-diameter mirrors on the wall to the rear of the rotating barber chairs. The only curious thing regarding the placement of these mirrors is that none of the mirrors lines up directly opposite any of the chairs, on either wall. The impact on you, and no doubt on all of Victor's other patrons, is that as you are getting your haircut your view is a section of gray wall directly centered between two large round mirrors, neither of which you can see yourself in. Each barber's chair at Victor's has the same arrangement of chairs juxtaposed with mirrors. Odd, you think to yourself, but maybe that's the way they did it in Romania, or wherever Victor is from.

Victor puts a hair poncho around your neck and snaps it. He snaps it on tightly just to show you who is boss, but tells you that it is to make sure that none of the hair he cuts falls down your shirt. Your son is patiently sitting directly behind you in a waiting chair. Victor, who likes your son, turns your chair around 180 degrees, to give you the benefit of looking at him. On this opposite wall, you have several three-foot-diameter mirrors that are, as on the front wall, positioned to the left and right of your field of vision. You cannot see yourself in any mirror on any wall. You conclude from this arrangement of chairs juxtaposed with mirrors that this haircut will be a surprise until the end, a fact that you accept with confidence, because your wife has recommended Victor.

Victor now begins to work his craft on your head. He starts from the bottom on the sides and back—"Just like building a house," you think he says to you, but you are not so sure because of his thick accent. "You work it from the bottom to the top." He is cutting and tilting and holding your head on one side, then the other. All of this is much different from Sandi's more gentle approach, but you assume that the difference in Victor's style is due to the hair training he may have received in Russia, Romania, or somewhere like that.

During this haircut, you look mostly at your son. The alternative is a section of gray wall that is the space between two round mirrors that are located in such a way that they do not reflect your image. You make funny faces at each other and try to make each other laugh. Your son, during this haircut, is a silent observer.

Victor announces to you that he is done. No last-minute touches here. No holding the mirror behind your head and reflecting it into the mirror in front of you, because that mirror is not located so that you can see yourself in it.

You emerge from your chair after Victor disrobes you of your hair smock, which frees up your breathing to full capacity, and you walk over to your son. He is laughing. You ask him what he is laughing about and he says nothing. He is too polite to reveal his thoughts in front of Victor. You look in the mirror and realize that this is the worst haircut that you have ever gotten in your life. It is shorter than you have had your hair in the past thirty-two years and you are the first to admit how goofy it looks. After your inspection, you conclude that there is no way that Victor can improve upon this unique cut that he has just given you; there is not enough hair left to work with. And besides that, his next customer has already been seated in the mirrorless chair from which you just emerged and is getting his smock wrapped too tightly around his neck, just like it was around yours. You pay Victor and leave him a generous tip so that he is nice to your son the next time he gets a buzz cut. The tip is in no way a reward for the great job he did on your head.

On the way home, your son, who is sitting diagonally behind you in the car, begins to ridicule you and call you "oval head." You ask why he did not say anything during this haircut to indicate to you that it was moving in the wrong direction. He says, "I don't know." Four minutes later, you arrive home and step in the back door to be greeted by your wife, whose outlook on these matters is always overly optimistic, especially when she has a stake in the recommendation process, as she did with Victor, so you expect positive feedback from her. But she says, "Oh, my God! What happened? What did you do to your head?" Your worst fears have just been confirmed as she tells you that you have an oval head. You received the worst possible haircut that you could have gotten. It is way worse than the shaggy hair that you walked into Victor's with.

You look at yourself in the mirror now in the privacy of your own home, where you can take the time to really inspect Victor's work. You cannot do this in the barbershop because you don't want Victor or his patrons to get the idea that you are a hair boy. You realize that it is bad and that nothing can be done. You concur with your son and your wife. You do, in fact, have an oval head.

Your daughter emerges from her bedroom, where she just put her eighteen dolls to sleep, and looks at you. "Daddy, you got a bad haircut. You have an oval head," she says innocently. You wait until ten minutes before you have to get in the limo to leave for the airport before starting to pack. You go. For the entire ride to the airport, each member of your family ridicules you for the funny-shaped head that you have and for the bad haircut that you came home with.

Lucky you, Mr. Oval Head. You are on the way to a family reunion. You cannot wait to see everyone.

Park Your Car

Your wife is on a health kick and she is enjoying going to the gym on a regular and frequent basis. Like you and the rest of your family, your wife belongs to a full-service gym, located in the suburb that is to the immediate south of your suburb. It is the gym that you bring your son to each Saturday for his glorious swim lessons with Annika. That suburb is much hipper and more citylike than your suburb. There are single people without kids living in that suburb, in large part due to the fact that there is a major university located in that town along beautiful Lake Michigan.

Because that suburb is a little like a suburb and a little like a city, the gym does not have its own parking lot. People who drive to this gym usually park on the street, as they say.

The parking situation outside of the gym is unique. The street is wide and the parking is angled toward the curb. The spots are striped. If you were parking there, you would pull into the curb with your front wheel. The parking spots are at, let's say, a thirty-degree angle, so that only one wheel touches the curb when you pull into your space. The spaces are angled so that when you are driving on the right side of the road you can easily pull into the angle of the parking spot. If, for instance, you were making a left-hand turn into the space, you would have to overcompensate for the reverse angle of the diagonal parking spaces so that you could get in. Unless you are a very skilled driver, it is difficult to pull directly into one of these diagonal spots when you are making a left-hand turn from the opposite side of the street, especially if cars are parked adjacent to the empty spot that you want.

Each of these spaces is metered, another sign that this suburb is different from yours. The gym is a popular gym and many people drive to it. It is always busy and it seems that no matter what time you show up, even if it's 5:30 A.M., the parking spaces in front of the gym are filled. A funny thing about gyms is that people go to them to do things like run on a treadmill for forty-five minutes yet they don't want to park more than a two-minute walk away.

So on this Wednesday morning, like most Wednesday mornings, your wife makes sure that your son makes it out to the bus stop OK and gets off to school. Your daughter does not have pre-school today because she is in the three-day-a-week program your wife signed her up for. Today is an off day for her. Your wife then loads your daughter into the Land Rover and off they go to the gym. Your daughter is excited to go to the gym day care, which your wife refers to as Fun Club, a term that she invented to give your daughter the idea that gym day care should actually be fun. On this morning, the psychology seems to be working, as your daughter is not crying.

On the way to the gym, the bright-yellow gas-tank light goes on, indicating that the Land Rover, which is the least fuel-efficient SUV on the face of the earth, has a very limited amount of premium-grade gas in it. Your wife sees this familiar light and, as usual, thinks that there is probably enough gas to get to the gym and back and that therefore she doesn't need to deal with the gas station now. As she approaches the gym, your wife notices the one and only spot that is available within two blocks of the gym. It is cold outside and that available spot is valuable. She races toward it while trying not to burn her last ounces of premium gasoline. The spot is *not* on the right side of the street but is on the left side, which means that she must wait for the four oncoming cars to pass her before she overcompensates her turn in order to efficiently pull into the only available, reverse-angled parking space. She stops, puts on her left-hand turn signal, and waits for the four oncoming cars to pass. This is the modern-day equivalent of a wolf marking its territory with urine, a demarcation that all animals know not to violate. While waiting for the four oncoming cars to pass, your wife explains to your four-year-old daughter how she scored with rock-star parking, an insider's joke she has with her friends, which your four-year-old is not as quick to pick up on as they would be.

Your wife waits patiently, because in the suburbs, even this one, people drive slowly. Three cars go past, and, as the fourth approaches, that driver, without putting on her directional, slips her minivan into the space that your wife has been patiently waiting for, with her directional flashing. Your wife cannot believe that this minivan-driving mom budged her, to lift an expression from your eight-year-old, and took the spot that was rightfully hers. She is pissed.

Your wife puts the Land Rover in park, leaving the car in the middle of the street, and jumps out to confront this overzealous mom who scored "her" rock-star spot. By the time your wife gets over to the other mom, she has just placed her second quarter in the parking meter. Abiding by the rules of screwing someone while driving, she avoids all eye contact with your wife and any acknowledgment that your wife, the person she just screwed over, even exists. Your wife gets within speaking range of the minivan mom as she is dropping her fourth quarter in the meter. "You took my parking spot," she says. "What do you mean, *your* parking spot?" the other mom retaliates. "The spot that you are in now, the one that I was waiting for with my turn signal on," your wife replies.

To which the other mom replies, "Well, that doesn't mean anything. You can't make a left-hand turn into a reverse-angled parking spot; you have to approach these spots from the side of the street that you are driving on." She says this with an authority that sounds like she knows something that your wife doesn't.

"That's bullshit," your wife says, loud enough for your preschool-aged daughter, who is still in the car, which is now parked in the middle of the street, to hear. "I was waiting for the space and it is mine; besides, my daughter is sick with a fever and there are no other spaces nearby. I do not want to expose her to the cold." (By the way, that morning, half an hour earlier, when you left the house for work, you detected no trace of sickness whatsoever.)

The other mom, not to be deterred, retaliates by looking at her daughter, who is still sitting in her car, and says, "So? My daughter has diabetes; she has difficulty walking, so I have to park close to the gym." At a loss for a rational rebuttal, but nevertheless undeterred from retaliating, your wife, whose veins are protruding from her muscular neck, says, "Oh yeah? My mother is dead and my father has acrophobia."

The other mom puts her fifth quarter in the meter, avoids further eye contact with your wife, and walks with her twenty-five-year-old diabetic "child" into the gym. Your wife gets back in the Land Rover and slams the door. She continues driving and secures the first available spot she sees, three blocks away, which no one would describe as rock-star parking. On the long, cold walk to the gym, she tries to come up with an answer to your daughter's two questions: "What happened to our rock-star parking, Mommy?" and "Why did you get so mad at that lady?" Your wife has ten minutes to answer these questions before your daughter gets dropped off at Fun Club.

Try to Make a Phone Call

You come home from work and you are at the front door struggling to find the key, which you have probably misplaced, and you see your wife through the window. She is talking on the phone. You try to get her attention by waving, but she is engrossed in her conversation. You ring the bell and you can tell by her expression that she is distracted and annoyed by the doorbell ringing. She opens the door without interrupting her phone conversation. She does not have the time to acknowledge you, except for the fact that she is annoyed because you disturbed her train of thought during her important phone conversation.

You put your briefcase down and hug your kids. You head upstairs to change your clothes and you tell them that you will be right down. You want to change out of your tailor-reinforced wholesale suit. This is the first thing you like to do each and every night when you get home, after greeting everyone, because it somehow transitions you from being a corporate executive to being a dad and husband and regular guy, a guy who is ready to hang out with his family.

You come downstairs and your wife whispers to you, while still on the phone, "I am just wrapping up, honey." You notice the pasta in the large pot of boiling water and it is all floating on the top. A bad sign. A sign of overcooked, limp noodles. You race to the rescue, because your wife is too busy with her important conversation to be bothered with matters as small as the pasta noodles that you are about to eat for supper. Your son and daughter both see you take control of the cooking pasta and ask if they can test the noodles, a skill that you have trained them well at, a skill that they can rely on for their entire lives because they, unlike your wife, can discern a perfectly cooked noodle. The only downside is that, when a noodle is not boiled to perfection, they know and it bothers them.

You lift a limp noodle out of the pot of water, and at that moment you know what each of their reactions will be. As you move the noodle away from the pot of water, you mentally craft the strategy that you will use this evening to try to deceive your children into believing that the noodles will taste good once they are smothered in red sauce. You have a difficult time convincing them of this because you cannot convince yourself of it, and, like you, they know a perfectly cooked noodle. The only person in your family these overcooked noodles will not matter to is your wife. She has prepared some low-carb dish for herself.

You empty the pasta pot into the colander, drain the water, and empty the pasta into a bowl that your wife placed on the counter before you arrived home. You smother it with red sauce.

You serve the pasta on the plates on the table and have the kids sit down. You look at your wife with an annoyed expression and she looks at you with an expression that says, "I am on an important call, one that cannot be disturbed for something as trivial as sitting down together to eat dinner." Sometime you would like your wife to pay attention to you like she does to whoever is on the other end of this call. You and the kids start eating and your wife hangs up. She joins you.

"Who was that?" you ask. "Oh, it was Jessica. We are arranging swim class for the girls." You are amazed by this call and others like it for two reasons. First of all, in the fifteen minutes or so of your wife's phone conversation that you partially overheard you did not hear any discussion whatsoever about swimming. Second, you know that if it were you arranging swim lessons for your daughter and her friend the call would go something like this: "Hey, Bill, what's up? Hey, I was thinking we should get the kids in swim class. What do you think?" "I know a really good swim teacher. Her name is Annika. I'll set it up for Saturday." "See ya."

In that hypothetical conversation, you have arrived at a conclusion every bit as good as your wife's, only she has taken twenty-two minutes to do it and you took twenty-one seconds.

You are just finishing dinner and it is time to begin clearing the table and washing the dishes. The phone rings. You look at caller ID, knowing that there is no chance that this call is for you. You are right. It is Findley, Susan. Perfect timing. You hand your wife the phone, and while you, your son, and daughter clear the table, rinse the dishes, stack the dishwasher, clean the countertops and kitchen table, and sweep the floor, your wife is working through the details of having Max over tomorrow after school for a playdate, details that must be discussed immediately after dinner during cleanup rather than, say, during the day, when both your wife and Susan are home without kids.

Your wife has another two calls to make about the school benefit, which she is organizing. These are not brief calls, because there is no such thing as a brief call with your wife. There are many, many very important details to discuss. Everything must be perfect.

You hang out with the kids and play with them. You try not to make too much noise with them, because this will get your wife upset while she is on the phone. Rather than her moving to another room to continue her conversation, she will point her finger at a forty-five-degree angle upward, indicating that she wants you to take the kids upstairs so that you don't distract her while she's on her call.

The phone rings again and the caller ID says Jaynor, Richard, a name that you do not recognize. While the phone is ringing, you hand it to your wife and she says that it is Sue from book club. Another twenty-five-minute discussion. "Sue needed to know what book we were reading this month," your wife says after hanging up.

Again, the phone rings and you try something that you rarely attempt. You answer the phone without looking at the caller ID. It is Beth. "Hang on a minute, Beth," you say politely. "Let me get Diane for you." After climbing two flights of stairs to find your wife, you indicate to her that Beth is on the phone, and she looks at you with an annoyed expression. She does not feel like talking on the phone and implies, with her annoyed facial expression, that you were somehow supposed to know that. You can tell by your wife's expression that you must tell Beth that your wife is busy putting your daughter to bed and that she will give her a call back. How can you be so stupid as to assume that your wife wanted to talk on the phone with Beth?

Later that night, you listen to the message machine to hear that your father left a message for you earlier that day. You have one call to return, an important one. Your father wants to check up on his stock portfolio, which you manage for him. You reach for your Blackberry, where you have his phone number, and then reach for the phone.

"What are you doing?" your wife asks. "I am calling my father back." "Now?" she says. "Yes, I need to talk with him for one minute"—the average length of the few calls a week you make from home. "He wants to know if I purchased General Dynamics for him today." "What about the kids? Are you going to ignore the kids? They haven't seen you all day long," she says.

You sheepishly put the phone down and know that you will have to make this thirty-second call after the kids are asleep. You hang out with the kids and put your son to bed. Your wife puts your daughter to bed. You emerge from your son's room and reach for the phone. You pick it up to hear your wife on the phone downstairs. You put the phone back in the cradle and accept that you will return your father's call tomorrow from work.

So Tell Me All About Your Thong Underwear

You and your wife attend an evening fund-raiser for an organization that you will call Kids First. Of the many fund-raisers that you attend annually, this one is the most fun because almost everyone who lives in your suburb comes out to support the event. It is a big neighborhood party at the local club.

You show up at the event, and every which way you turn there are ways to spend money. You already dropped a few hundred dollars on the admission tickets. There are raffle tickets for bicycles, opportunities for kids to be Chicago Cubs bat boys for a day, shopping sprees at Nike Town, and hundreds of other items, which for the most part you do not pay attention to because you have been drinking beer and wine and hanging out with all of your friends. Besides, you have "won" enough items at prior fund-raisers to know that tomorrow the items you fight hard to pay outrageously for tonight will seem ridiculous to you, largely due to the two beers and two glasses of red wine that will impair your buying judgment.

Tonight, most of the people whom you hang out with are guys, because tonight they, like you, are trying to avoid any additional cash outlay during this economically challenging time. You all know, however, that your wives are spending their time determining the best items for you to "win" that evening. You will better understand how your wife spent her evening when you stop by the checkout table on your way out.

Every two years, Kids First elects a president, an upstanding volunteer from the community, to do, well, you are not sure exactly what. During the current term, the president is a woman whom you know and enjoy joking around with named Lynne O'Donnell. That evening, Lynne told you that the Kids First presidency was not all that it was cracked up to be and that, going in, she thought that she could have more impact on the organization than she was actually able to. "Kids First does not like change," she tells you. "They only want to maintain the status quo."

It is interesting, you think, that Lynne has revealed herself to you in that way, because you know Lynne to be a person who does not like to say negative things, even when she has negative thoughts. You think that Lynne has revealed herself to you in this manner because, like you, she may have had two beers and two glasses of wine.

You break away from your conversation with Lynne and find yourself standing alone in a corridor outside the bidding room, waiting for your wife to place her final "winning" bid on two Cubs baseball game tickets. "Can you believe that I got the tickets for only $410?" she says excitedly, as though she has just won something.

Lynne approaches you while you are standing in the corridor outside the bidding room. She is feeling guilty for expressing a negative thought to you three minutes earlier and apologizes for being a negative person. You think she tells you this because she feels guilty. You did not really take notice of, nor would you probably remember, the conversation tomorrow, but now that you suspect that Lynne feels guilty about revealing a negative thought to you, you can joke with her about this so that she will never forget. She makes you swear that you will not tell anyone.

Lynne, looking for something to do with her nervous energy while feeling overwhelmed with guilt, slips her right hand, so that it almost fully disappears, inside the front of her pants and pulls out a business card–size piece of card stock, which was sandwiched between her skin and her skin-hugging pants, with the number 37 written on it. Your eyes involuntarily follow the movements of her right hand as she does this.

With that, you ask Lynne—the thin, in-shape, skin-tight short shirt and skin-tight pant wearing, flat-and-exposed tummy Kids First president—"What exactly was securing that card with the number 37 written on it between you and your pants?" because you didn't really notice any visible means of support for the card. You then realize that you did notice a thin strap of white fabric, so you continue your inquiry, asking the president of Kids First a question that you know would embarrass her had she not consumed the beer and wine that you suspect she has. "Is that a thong you are wearing?" you ask, expecting her to ignore you. "Yes, it is," she says with pride, smiling a thong-wearing smile because you have discovered something about her that she tells you not even her husband is aware of.

Well, all of a sudden this fund-raiser has gotten a hell of a lot more interesting for you. "Why bother?" you ask. "Isn't it uncomfortable?"—equating it to a wedgie, something to which you can relate. While wondering who else among you is wearing a thong tonight, you ask, "Doesn't it feel like you are being crept up upon?" trying desperately to think of anything to say to keep this conversation from dying.

As your blond, long-haired, in-shape, skin-tight-outfit-wearing, quick-witted wife walks over to ask you for your credit card, she realizes immediately that you and the Kids First president are discussing the features and benefits of thong underwear, and when she does she reveals to you and the Kids First president that she too is wearing a thong, a fact that you wish you had been previously aware of. This fund-raiser has now just gotten twice as good as it was ten minutes earlier, and ten minutes earlier it was pretty damn good. To you and your wife, Lynne offers that the main benefit of the thong is that there is no VPL, a fact with which your wife concurs. Then, to you, they both demonstrate what they are talking about. It is a demonstration that you enjoy, and one that will make the $410 baseball tickets and whatever else you have "won" that night seem like a good value, even tomorrow. Not taking this conversation quite as far as you would have liked to, you reluctantly break away and head over to the checkout table. "Let's go," your wife says.

From this evening forward, you have a newfound appreciation for all the responsibility that comes with the position of the Kids First presidency. This school fund-raiser, with this Kids First president, you come to realize, is one that you will never, ever forget for as long as you live.

This evening, you go home and have sex with your wife.

A week after the Kids First fund-raiser, where you discovered that the thin, in-shape, tight-pants- and short-tight-shirt-wearing Kids First president wears thong underwear, and after doing so were able to so brilliantly engage her in a lengthy discussion on the topic, you attend a birthday party for some friends of yours, a couple, who are both turning forty that month. This is a fun, informal fortieth-birthday party where alcohol is being served, people are *not* standing up at a microphone to share their feelings about the forty-year-olds, and everyone knows one another. It is a good time.

You are talking with John, a friend of yours, about skiing, one of your favorite topics and his, especially when it involves

Jackson Hole or Telluride, and out of the corner of your eye during this ski/snowboard/Telluride/Jackson Hole discussion you see Lynne, your Kids First president. She is wearing a skin-tight fitting outfit, no VPL, and her flat tummy is exposed. From afar, you become curious about her conversation, whatever it might be about, and you prematurely conclude your ski conversation with John to "go get a refill," even though your glass is not empty. "Excuse me," you say to John, "I'll be right back"—knowing that you are going to continue the thong-underwear discussion that you started only one week ago with Lynne, the Kids First president, who is off-duty tonight. You do not expect to see John for the rest of the evening.

You see that Lynne is holding an almost empty margarita glass, a good sign, you think, that your conversation with her will be more interesting than any ski talk.

On the way over to the professionally staffed bar, you just happen to walk by Lynne. "Oh, Lynne," you say as spontaneously as you can, given the planning that went into this encounter. "How are you doing?" She is talking with two other people and she sort of breaks away from her conversation with them to talk with you, or that's what you think, anyway. You give Lynne a knowing smile, like you are sharing her thong-wearing secret with her, and she looks at you with a "Stop smiling at me like that, you creep" expression.

Your main interest in talking with Lynne at this moment is to rekindle the intriguing conversation that was so abruptly ended at the school fund-raiser last weekend.

Explaining the smirk that is on your face and trying to open the door to the last and most interesting conversation you have ever had with Lynne, you ask, "So, Lynne, tell me, are you wearing a thong tonight?"

She looks at you and she does not smile. In fact, her facial expression changes from carefree to concerned or puzzled; no, make that pissed off, like you said something entirely inappropriate, or like you did not pull over to the side of the road to let her pass. "What are you talking about?" she asks, in a manner that suggests you have offended her. You laugh, knowing that Lynne is just goofing you, but her expression does not change and she is really pissed off. You can tell that she is not messing around.

"Lynne, do you remember our conversation at the Kids First fund-raiser on Saturday?" "You were there?" she says, in a surprised manner, adding, "I didn't see you there. Wasn't it so great this year?" "It was terrific," you reply. "In fact, it was the best Kids First fund-raiser that I have ever attended. I learned so much about the management of Kids First." "We raised $260,000—isn't that incredible!" Lynne exclaims. "It has been such a rewarding year to be involved with Kids First. We made a lot of great changes this year."

In your peripheral vision, you see John and excuse yourself from Lynne. You quickly make your way back to John. "So, John, isn't Corbet's Couloir one of the hairiest runs that you have ever skied?"

EPILOGUE

Your friend, neighbor, and baseball co-coach, who is a Hollywood screenwriter, writes and has published a letter to the editor in your local newspaper, a newspaper that is circulated to subscribers that reside in your suburb and the wealthier suburb to the immediate north of your suburb. His letter to the editor, like the Christmas cards this guy writes, is very funny. It is filled with funny stories that support his basic premise that a two-week winter school vacation is way too long. Over that period the kids start driving everyone crazy. He writes that it has gotten so bad that he gives each of his kids $50 and sends them off on their bikes to a shopping mall that is twenty miles from where he lives, just to get them out of the house. He is, of course, joking, and you laugh when you read his letter. In your mind, it warrants a thoughtful response, especially after you heard that some people had called him, upset, thinking that he was serious and that he was really starting to drink more.

One morning at two o'clock you wake up out of a sound sleep with an idea for a response to his letter. Your idea is to write what a great vacation you had with your family because you did so many worthwhile things with your kids. You hyperbolize, like you have throughout this book, about things you did over the vacation and write about them in a way that you think is very funny. That next evening, you type this letter into your computer, print it out, and read it to your wife, who is usually fairly reserved when you read to her all the funny e-mails and thank-you notes that you write. She laughs uncontrollably. She has sex with you that night.

The next morning, Saturday, you tune it up, print it out, and while on your run you drop it off at your friend's. You choose *not* to submit it to the editorial department of your suburban paper because you are not sure that everyone who lives in your suburb will understand your humor and you don't want to expose yourself in that manner to your entire suburb, like you have here.

When you return from your run, your friend and his wife are on the phone with your wife. You don't realize this at first, but then your wife hands you the phone. They are laughing and tell you that they thought your letter was funny. To you, this is a big compliment. Your friend has written a bunch of big-time Hollywood movies; he is a neighborhood celebrity; he knows funny writing, and he is on the phone complimenting you on your letter. His wife concurs. They moved to your suburb from Hollywood. They are your friends. And you have made them laugh with something you wrote.

You e-mail a lot, mostly because you have a portable device called a Blackberry, which allows you to send and receive e-mails anywhere. Frequently you send what you think are funny e-mails. Sometimes people even tell you that your e-mails are funny (but not as often as you write them). You even compile a book of your funniest e-mails at the end of the year and give it to your friend-boss. He tells you they are funny, and his wife has told you repeatedly that you should write a book of travel stories, because you travel a lot and some e-mails that she has read, that you have written, make her laugh.

You think on that and the next day, which is a Sunday, you start to make a list of humorous events based on your life in the suburbs. For each instance, you think of a story and you start laughing. You start writing these stories down, and as you do so, you exaggerate them, and laugh some more. They come easily and seem to pour out of you. To you they are as funny as the events you described in that letter to your friend. One reason you think that these situations are so funny is that your stories are told from a guy's perspective, a perspective that is often neglected in your suburb.

The next day, Monday, you travel to New York. You return on Tuesday and on Wednesday you are off to Montreal. You have been writing since Sunday, when you have the time, like from 4 to 6:30 A.M., and 9 P.M. to midnight, and you think that this book idea of yours is materializing. It is jelling. It is happening. It's yours.

You arrive home from Montreal and pull up to your house at 5:30 P.M. in the car that usually picks you up at the airport. You walk in the house and like many times when you enter a room that your wife is in, she seems startled. This puzzles you, but she is happy to see you and you are happy to see her.

As you are taking your coat off, your wife informs you that she has an idea. This is an introduction that you have heard before and an introduction that usually ends up costing you money. It is the same introduction that initiated the $1,600 kids' bathroom ceiling painting project. You exercise the active listening skills that you learned when you were a Camp Tamarack counselor and say, "You have an idea, honey?" She says, "Yes, I have an idea. I was thinking that we can write the book together."

You dwell on this surprising thought of hers for a minute or two before you respond. First, you cannot think of one book with which you are familiar that was written by two authors. Second, you have an image of this book as being your own project, one of the few things in your life that you can call your own. Third, your idea is to make sure that the guy's (*your*) perspective surfaces in the book; that is one of the reasons why this book will be funny. You have visions of what it would be like writing a book with the same woman who has redecorated your front hallway entryway table in such a way that you can no longer find your Blackberry, keys, cell phone, and wallet and that every time you need to look for something you must search through five clasped ornamental boxes that sit on the entryway table, one of which has been turned backward because your wife didn't think that the front of it was attractive. The same woman who wants to attach herself to your project has relocated your running shoes to a place that you, in a million years, would have never thought of, because one day she did not think that they looked good in the place where you had kept them for the preceding 1,780 days.

You know your wife well and know that she had given this idea of coauthoring your book a lot of thought. She has also considered how she would approach you so that you would be most receptive to the concept of her coauthorship. She wants in. She wants your book to be her book too. She does not want to be left out.

She notices your hesitation to verbalize your thoughts and feelings, which is a common hesitation each time you are asked to express your feelings. She adds, "I just thought that it would be a fun and romantic thing that we could do together." To which you quickly reply, "If you are looking for something fun and romantic that we could do together for the next several months, why don't we just have a lot of sex?"

She tells you that she is overly tired and is tapped out from the demands that the kids place on her all day long, or at least when they are not in school seven hours each day. Emphatically, you tell your wife that you know that she has an important job with the kids and that you understand why she doesn't want to have sex. You know that if you had to deal with the demands of your kids from 7:30 to 8:30 every morning and from 3:30 to 6 every evening, with the rest of the day all to yourself, that you too would be too "tapped out" to have sex. She has a demanding job, you know.

You look at your wife and say, "Honey, I would love to work with you on this project, but this is something that I really have to do on my own." She says, "Well, it was just an idea." You do not have sex that night.